Attitude
Is Everything

10 Life-Changing Steps
to Turning Attitude Into Action

KEITH HARRELL

HarperBusiness
An Imprint of HarperCollinsPublishers

This book is dedicated with the greatest love, and affection to my family and friends for their love, support, and encouragement. And most important, to God for giving me everything—life, knowledge, wisdom, and the ability to do His work.

The Leah Friedman quote which appears on page 198 originally appeared in *On Women Turning 70: Honoring the Voices of Wisdom*, edited by Cathleen Rountree. Copyright © 1999 by Jossey Bass, Inc., San Francisco, California, a subsidiary of John Wiley & Sons, Inc., New York. Used by permission of the publisher. All Rights Reserved.

The Charles R. Swindoll quote on page 131 originally appeared in *Strengthening Your Grip*, by Charles R. Swindoll. Copyright © 1982 Word, Inc., Nashville, Tennessee. All rights reserved. Used by permission of Insight for Living, Anaheim, California 92806.

HarperCollins books may be purchased for educational, business, or sales promotional use. For information please write: Special Markets Department, HarperCollins Publishers Inc., 10 East 53rd Street, New York, NY 10022.

First HarperBusiness paperback edition published 2003

Designed by Lindgren/Fuller Design

Library of Congress Cataloging-in-Publication Data has been applied for.

ISBN 0-06-019605-X
ISBN 0-06-095490-6 (pbk.)

03 04 05 06 07 ❖/RRD 10 9 8 7

CONTENTS

ACKNOWLEDGMENTS

I was blessed to have the help and support of many talented people to whom I want to express my sincere thanks:

To my wonderful staff, Joyce Head, Sandi Miller, and Heidi Stepanovitch, for all their help and support.

To Diane Reverand, my editor, for her insight, feedback and expertise, and Janet Dery, Richard Rhorer and the other wonderful staff at HarperCollins.

To my literary agent Jan Miller who shared my vision and enthusiasm for this book and pushed to help make it a reality.

To Wes Smith for your tireless and committed effort, for taking my thoughts and ideas and building a foundation on which this manuscript was built. This project couldn't have been done without you.

To my sister Toni Malliet for your guidance and support. When I need you you always come through.

Special thanks to my friend Arabella Grayson for your countless hours, insight, enduring support, and positive attitude throughout this entire project. I thank God for you.

And finally, to the many individuals who have in their own special ways contributed to the creation of this book: Cherie Carter-Scott, Ph.D; Joy Carver, Dan Clark, Ron Cox, Beverly Forte, Ph.D.; Reggie Green, Daelyn Gruenberg, Hattie Hill, Janet Hill, Sam Horn, Clove Hoover, Kathy Jeremiah, Steve and Kelly Lynn Pipkin, Ellen Joan Pollack, Mark Seal, Doug Smart, Colandra Wright, and Carolyn Zatto.

PREFACE TO THE
PAPERBACK EDITION

Attitude is 100 percent of everything you do!

After more than two decades of speaking to people about the power of attitude, I know that a positive attitude is your most priceless possession, one of your most valuable assets. To a great extent, it determines the overall quality of your life.

Attitude Is Everything grew out of my desire to share the truths I've learned about the life-transforming power of attitude with individuals who will never have an opportunity to hear me speak at corporate conferences and national conventions. Since it was first published in 2000 the world as we once knew it has been irrevocably changed. For many of us, events of September 11, major corporate scandals, the economic downturn and the constant threat of terrorism have shattered our ideals and caused us to lose confidence in institutions we once respected.

In this climate of uncertainty, I am convinced more than ever that people need to know how to control and manage the quality of their lives through a positive mental attitude. It's no secret that life seems to reward us most when we approach the world with a positive attitude. But somehow this knowledge escapes us when we experience a setback or encounter adversity.

I am often asked if a person's attitude is predisposed or if it can be developed. Without question, attitudes are developed. The great psychologist-philosopher William James said, "The greatest discovery of my generation is that people can alter their lives by altering their attitudes of mind." I can say that one of the greatest realizations of our time is that everyone has the potential to improve the quality of their personal and professional lives; however, they must first be willing to acquire the skills that will guide them to a place of self-discovery where they can tap into the power of their positive attitude. *You may not be able to change your height or your body type, but you can change your attitude*. Each of us has the power to develop and maintain a positive attitude that works for us, that improves the quality of our lives and enables us to accomplish our life objectives. Your attitude should be an indication of where you desire to go in life and not a reflection of what you've been through. Change your attitude and you can change your life!

No matter how old you are, your current position or station in life, your gender, or marital status, a positive attitude can make an incredible difference in your life and in the lives of others. In the chapters that follow, I give you the tools you need to develop and maintain a positive attitude; the *ten steps for turning attitude into action* focus on the fundamental principles of self-development and personal growth. The theme that runs through these steps, like a single strand through fabric, is that in learning to monitor and control your attitude, you can begin to increase the quality of your personal and professional life.

As you step out to enrich your life, allow *Attitude Is Everything* to be your blueprint. By applying the principles you have a daily resource and support system that will provide you with enhanced step-by-step instructions for improving the overall quality of your personal and professional life.

Remember that real wealth is measured not by what you have, not by where you are, but by the spirit that lives within you. Success *is* an attitude. I wish you a super-fantastic journey as you discover that Attitude . . . is everything.

Keith Harrell
September 2002

INTRODUCTION

*Your attitude today determines
your success tomorrow.*

THE SELLING OF A GOLDEN SPEECH: ON THE MOTIVATIONAL CIR-
CUIT, A STAR WITH ATTITUDE read the headline of a feature article in the *Wall Street Journal*. The article was about attitude
and the positive effect I was having on hundreds of organizations and thousands of individuals around the world. The
topic of the "golden speech" was "Attitude Is Everything."
The article confirmed what I already knew, that people and
organizations today, more than ever before, need to learn
how to manage and control the quality of their lives through
the power of a positive attitude. I am humbled each and
every time someone mentions this article, but I am also
reminded of the powerful impact of attitude. Attitude is the
foundation and support of everything we do, a key element
in the process of controlling your destiny and achieving mastery in your personal and professional life.

Over the years, I've attended countless seminars, read
hundreds of books, listened to hours and hours of tapes, and
interviewed scores of successful people on the subject of
self-development. I've discovered that learning to monitor,
control, and tap into a positive attitude is the key to every

self-help process. In fact, *the most valuable asset you can possess is a positive attitude toward your life.* It isn't how much you know about maintaining a positive attitude that's important; it's how well, and how consistently, you put that knowledge to use.

Your attitude is often one of the first things people notice about you. You may not be able to change your height or your body type, but you can change your attitude. Many researchers believe—and I wholeheartedly agree—that a positive attitude is not a product of genetics and heredity but, with proper training, an acquired trait. The best thing about your attitude is that if it's bad, it can be made better, and if it's good, it can be made even greater.

Each of us has the power to choose a positive attitude over a negative one. If you want an attitude that works for you, that improves the quality of your life and enables you to accomplish your dreams, you have to work at it. You can't just sit around and wait for a positive attitude to come over you. In this book, I will provide you with tools to tune and take control of your attitude, even in the most challenging times.

The material in this book is not merely motivational. It offers you step-by-step instructions and examples of how others—including myself—have benefited by taking responsibility for their attitudes. You have made an investment in yourself—an investment that will pay dividends when—and only when—you apply the principles and take action. The fundamental principle is that *attitude is everything.* You'll learn that no matter how old you are, what your position or station in life, your gender, or your marital status, a positive attitude can make an incredible difference.

In the chapters that follow, I will give you the tools you need for an attitude tune-up. I'm going to provide you with *ten steps for turning attitude into action.* Each of the steps focuses on fundamental principles of self-development and personal growth. The theme that runs through these steps, like a single strand through a fabric, is that in learning to monitor and control your attitude, you can make an incredible difference in your life and in the lives of people around you. Here is a brief description of each of the steps that will help you develop a super-fantastic attitude.

Step 1: Understand the Power of Attitude

Your attitude is a powerful tool for positive action. It's inherently interwoven into everything you do. It's your most priceless possession. The good news is, you don't have to buy it. But you do have to develop it. In the first chapter, you will discover what attitude is, the power of attitude, and how your attitude reflects you. You'll learn to recognize that you can control your destiny by learning the four things you need to do to stay positive even in the most challenging times.

Step 2: Choose to Take Charge of Your Life

To transform your attitude into action, you must accept responsibility for what goes on inside your mind by monitoring your internal dialogue. We will look at the power of *choice,* how your choices determine your happiness and affect your success. I will offer you the keys to controlling how you respond to whatever the world throws at you, by showing you how to monitor and manage your attitude.

Step 3: Identify through Self-Awareness the Attitudes That Hold You Back or Propel You Forward

By practicing *self-awareness,* you will learn the three types of bad attitudes. You will discover how to assess your present-day attitude by identifying the things that may be holding you back and to find the attitude needed to propel you forward. You will look at the underlying causes of a bad attitude and discover how to shift turning points into learning points by taking an attitude assessment.

Step 4: Reframe Your Bad Attitude

An attitude of anger can be transformed into an attitude of gratitude and forgiveness by shifting your perspective. You will discover the power of self-forgiveness, which allows you to forgive others. You will also learn how to recognize and rid yourself of a debilitating attitude by identifying the three P's that cause a bad attitude.

Step 5: Find Your Purpose and Passion

Once you've determined what has been holding you back, it's time to look ahead and analyze where you want to go. Understanding the importance of living your life with *purpose* and *passion*—having a personal vision—is critical to achieving success. You will consider which attitudes are conducive to goal-setting and which can spoil the process. And finally, I will explain the strategy of creating a personal and professional life plan.

Step 6: Be Pre-Active

In this step, you will learn to prepare yourself for those times when challenging circumstances threaten to provoke negative attitudes that can hinder your plans and throw you off course en route to your goals and dreams. You will discover that even with a positive attitude, purpose, and passion, life is never without challenges, disappointments, setbacks, and problems. By developing a pre-active approach to life, you will become better prepared to handle the hazards you face in life.

Step 7: Discover How to Motivate Yourself

You will discover the keys to self-motivation by making use of the Attitude Tool Kit: affirmations, visualization, attitude talk, positive greetings, enthusiasm, spiritual empowerment, humor, and exercise. By using your Attitude Tool Kit, you will be well equipped to seek personal and professional success.

Step 8: Build Supportive Relationships

Nobody makes it alone in this world. We all need supportive relationships to get through challenging times. In this chapter, I will help you put together your A-Team, those people who will help you fight off negative attitudes and build positive ones. To build a team, you first have to develop an attitude that will make others want to support you. I'll show you how to build long-term, mutually beneficial relationships through networking, shared vision, and shared values. You will also learn the best defense against toxic people who try to disrupt your success.

Step 9: See Change as an Opportunity

One of the greatest challenges to a positive attitude is *change*, whether it's a change of jobs, a change in a relationship, or a change in your economic status. We'll look at the benefits of adopting a *whatever-it-takes* attitude when confronted by change. You will also learn the characteristics of the change process, the four ways individuals respond to it, and ten strategies for embracing change.

Step 10: Leave a Lasting Legacy

Sometimes we forget that the greatest thing we can do to build a healthy attitude is to get involved in something greater than ourselves. In Step 10, you'll learn the benefit of planting positive seeds: seeds of hope, encouragement, faith, and love. In this final step, you will discover how you can leave a lasting legacy by making a mark that cannot be erased. You'll be ready to transcend yourself and reach out to make a difference in the lives of your family, friends, and community.

If you want a positive attitude, you're going to need to be committed enough to work at it. This book is a guide toward developing the positive attitude that will work for you. I will provide you with the information and the plan. It's up to you to provide the effort and discipline to put the plan into action. It will take some work on your part, but I promise you will get a wonderful return on your investment.

Although the process I've mapped out is not always easy, I have broken it into small bytes of information and small action steps to make your goals easier to reach. I've suggested little adjustments that can change your thinking in a big way. By changing your thinking, you can change your beliefs. By changing your beliefs, you can change your actions—and your life.

Remember, this is an investment in you. The light is green, so *go!* I wish you a *super-fantastic* journey as you discover the power of your attitude.

CHAPTER ONE

Attitude Is Everything

STEP 1
Understand the power of "attitude."

The first thing you need to do, to turn your attitude into action, is to tap into the power of your attitude. This key step is the foundation on which the other nine steps in this book are built. Attitude *is* everything; it impacts everything you do.

As far back as I can remember, I've heard about the importance of a positive attitude and the powerful effect it could have on my life. I heard it from my parents, teachers, coaches, and supervisors over the years. How many times in your life have you been encouraged to have a positive attitude? Although attitude plays an important role in everyone's life, many people don't know its meaning or realize the influence it has on their performance at work and on their relationships. What, then, is attitude?

The *American Heritage Dictionary* defines *attitude* as a state of mind or feeling with regard to some matter. For me, *attitude* can be defined in one word: *life*. The attitude that you carry around makes an incredible difference in your life. It can be a powerful tool for positive action. Or it can be a poison that cripples your ability to fulfill your potential. Your attitude dictates whether you are living life or life is living you. Attitude determines whether you are on the way or in the way.

I spent most of my young adulthood chasing a dream to become a professional basketball player. In high school, I was an All-American and the Most Valuable Player of our state championship team. I accepted a scholarship to Seattle University, where I was the team captain for three of my four years. I averaged more than sixteen points per game in my senior year. In June 1979 I expected to be drafted by a National Basketball Association team. It was a dream that I had shared with everyone I knew. My family, friends, teammates, and others who had followed my career had come to expect that it would happen, based on my success as a player in high school and college.

On the day of the NBA draft, I waited and waited and waited . . . but the phone did not ring. I was devastated. I had devoted myself to the sport and to my future as an NBA player. It was tough to give up on that dream. I felt cheated when it didn't happen.

In the days and weeks that followed, the bitterness was revived every time someone commented on my failure to be drafted. It didn't help when strangers would note my six-foot-six-inch height and say, "You must play pro basketball." For a long time I fought the bitterness. Finally I decided to let go of the negative feelings. I found a way to embrace this major change and focus on being positive instead. I realized that to grow inwardly I had to move on with my life.

I developed a new attitude and a new response to questions about my height. Not long ago, a woman seated next to me at a luncheon asked if I played with the NBA.

"Yes, I do," I replied. "I'm a first-round draft choice. I'm the most valuable player. I'm owner of the team, and we win the championship every year!"

"So you do play with the NBA?" she asked.

"Yes, I do. I play with my **N**atural-**B**orn **A**bilities, and I'm slam-dunking every day!"

I did recover my positive attitude, but it took a focused effort to reframe my perspective, which is one of the key things I'm going to teach you in this book.

Failing to be drafted by the NBA was one of the greatest disappointments in my life. It affected my attitude adversely, throwing me off track for months. I'm sure you have dealt with similar circumstances in which an emotionally charged change in your life throws you off course. It happens to everyone, and often during such challenging times, we develop a negative attitude without being aware of the effect it has on our actions.

After my name was not called in the NBA draft, I felt disconnected from life. My self-confidence and self-esteem took a dive. Worse yet, I didn't have a contingency plan. So after college graduation, it was *Welcome to the real world, Keith. Whatcha gonna do now?* I had been a high-profile athlete in my hometown. Many people had followed my career through high school and into college. It seemed that everywhere I went people wanted to know what I planned to do with my life. They shared my disappointment, and that further zapped my sense of self-worth. I'd been secure in my role as an athlete. Suddenly I didn't know what I wanted to do.

I did decide that I had to get away from Seattle, where everyone seemed to know me and my disappointments. So I did what every warm-blooded African-American male does when he's feeling down and out and needs to return to his roots.

I went to Alaska.

My Aunt Sue was working in Anchorage. She offered to get me a job with her boyfriend, a painter who had a contract at Elmendorf Air Force Base. Instead of going to the NBA rookie camp, I joined the painter's union as an apprentice in Alaska. But a rookie is a rookie. I'd never painted with anything but my fingers in kindergarten. It showed. I was so bad they wouldn't let me do any real painting. I just did the prepping. I was an apprentice paint-prepper and not a very good one at that. If I'd come to Alaska to build up my self-esteem and improve my attitude, it wasn't working. I hadn't really escaped all the questions about my future, either.

One day, I was slopping paint on myself and getting a little on a wall when an older guy in coveralls came up to me with a look of concern. "You don't know me, but I know you. I followed your basketball career ever since you were in high school," he said. He then asked me what I was doing in Alaska working as a painter.

"I'm trying to figure out what to do with my life."

He gave me a sour look and pointed his paintbrush at me like a weapon. "I'm disappointed in you," he scolded. "You were a fine basketball player and a good student from what I read. It looks to me like you've given up. Looks like you're just sitting here taking the easy route."

I needed a good shake, and this former fan obliged. He made me realize that it was time to bounce back, time to get on with life. The next day I went looking for that painter. Poor guy, he didn't know what hit him. "Let me tell you something. If you've been watching me, keep on watching, because I haven't given up on life. I've just been trying to fig-ure out what game I'm going to play next!"

The guy did me a huge favor. He made me realize that I'd taken on an attitude of defeat, and it was dragging me down. I boarded the next plane out of Alaska and headed back to Seattle. On the way, I came up with a plan. It was a borrowed plan, but it beat painting icicles for the rest of my life.

A New Attitude and a New Plan

My father had been a professor of business and accounting for thirty-six years at Seattle Community College. He had always pushed me to major in business or accounting because he said it offered stable employment. My first goal upon returning home was to show my dad that I could make it in business. I was determined to get a job and stick with it as long as he had.

I'd been very secure in my future as a professional ath-lete, but I felt that I'd blown it. This time, I decided, I'm going to get a job and stick with it all the way. Never one to shy away from a challenge, I set my sights on the big daddy of big business: Big Blue—IBM, the Fortune 500 company that loved to brag it had never laid off anyone who deserved to have a job.

My cousin Kenny Lombard, who had also been a college basketball player, landed at IBM in Seattle after college. He'd been there three years, and he was doing very well. I went to him to ask about opportunities at Big Blue. "Do you think I have what it takes to get a job with IBM too?"

"Yes," he said. "But it's not going to be easy. You have to be *ready* to work for a company like IBM."

IBM Boot Camp

Big Blue was not hiring at that point, but Kenny said I should start preparing immediately so I'd be ready when they did open the door for new hires. He told me to come to his house every Saturday morning and he would put me through some mock interviews to help get me whipped into IBM shape. He wasn't kidding about the *whipping* part.

You might think that your cousin would take it easy on you. Not Kenny. He made me jump through some high hoops. The first time I went to his house, he sent me home before we'd even started because he felt I wasn't dressed properly. I wore a suit, but it was sort of a *disco* suit. The shirt wasn't right. My shoes were blue suede. "This is a business. You look like you're ready to go out to a club," Kenny said sternly. "Don't come back until you're dressed for a business interview."

It was the first time I'd been thrown out of a relative's house for inappropriate attire. I got the point, and I appreciated his honesty. I was Kenny's "project." He worked me hard in the days and weeks that followed. He taught me a lot about maintaining a proper business attitude. He made me work on my communication and language skills. He cut the "street" out of my vocabulary. "Keith, there is a difference in how you talk to an IBM customer and how you talk to your buddy who owns the gas station!"

Kenny also worked on my posture, presentation, and poise. My cousin, God bless him, was serious about getting me ready. He also taught me the history of IBM, its reputation as the premiere training ground for sales and management executives, and the corporation's three basic beliefs. These were based on principles developed by its legendary founder, Thomas Watson, Sr., who believed in *respect for the individual, customer service, and the pursuit of excellence.*

Whenever I had a problem understanding an IBM concept, Kenny put it in terms I could more easily understand. He used analogies from basketball to make things clearer for me. During the mock interviews, he taught me to acknowledge my weaknesses and to focus on my strengths. Since I hadn't majored in business or worked for a big company before, I was weak in background experience and knowledge. But I had been captain of a basketball team, and from that experience I understood teamwork, competition, and leadership.

Fit with a New Attitude

I have a natural tendency to become obsessive about things once I identify goals. Kenny got me focused. Other people began to think I had lost my mind.

My mother said, "Everybody knows IBM isn't hiring. You're wasting your time. Get a job!"

My friends gave me a hard time: "Let's see, Kenny's got you dressing up in a suit at the crack of dawn every Saturday morning so you can go over to his house and play IBM applicant? *Get a grip, man!*"

They didn't bother me. By this time, I'd built up an unstoppable attitude. I was going to get hired by Big Blue because failure was not an option. I kept myself on track and focused on the possibilities for tomorrow, not the realities of the moment.

One day, Kenny brought in a friend who was an assistant to the regional manager for IBM. He interviewed me. He said he liked my confidence and my positive attitude. Then he did a little fine-tuning on my interviewing skills and told me he'd meet with me again in two weeks to see if I'd improved.

Adjust Your Attitude
and Change Your Life

I was becoming a fanatic about getting hired by IBM, just as I'd been about preparing myself for basketball. I was one of those guys who *slept* with his basketball. I tied my right hand behind my back so I'd learn to use my left. I was *ready* when the assistant to the regional manager from IBM came back. I was in the Big Blue Zone.

I caught and ran with everything he threw at me. My cousin had drilled me and drilled me, and I'd drilled myself some more. At the end of the second practice interview, the assistant pronounced me ready for prime time. He told me that IBM still was not hiring, but he offered to get me a "courtesy" interview within a week.

The interview was with Colby Sillers, an IBM manager in the sales division. He was an ex-Marine, though from his drill-sergeant demeanor you couldn't tell that he'd ever left boot camp. "You didn't take any business courses in college, Keith. What makes you feel like you qualify to come to work for IBM? What makes you qualified for a business like ours?"

I was prepared.

"Mr. Sillers, I spent four years in college. I graduated on time. I majored in community service. It taught me how to deal with all kinds of people and how to build and manage relationships. Today, you have to understand relationships, and I think I understand relationships better than anybody does. Now, the business thing—I have a great attitude. I can learn the business skills. I started on the senior varsity basketball team all four years in college, which proves I'm a hard worker. I was the team captain, which demonstrates my leadership abilities. I know about preparation and competition. I can handle anything IBM asks me to do."

Every potential weakness Sillers cited in my background, I turned into a strength that I could bring to the company. What really won him over, though, was how I fielded one of the key questions asked in job interviews by IBM, which is a company of masterful salespeople, founded by a legendary salesman.

"Keith, how would you sell me this pencil?" he asked.

"Mr. Sillers, before I sell you anything, let me take the time to understand exactly what your needs are because I want to sell you what you need, not what I think you need. So let me ask you a few questions. . . ."

I blew him away. The Marine surrendered. I took the hill.

That courtesy interview got me in the door. I sailed through a half-dozen more screenings, and the next thing I knew, there was someone on the phone one morning saying, "Congratulations. Your first day of work at IBM is October 17."

My cousin Kenny had taught me a lot, but the most important lesson I learned was that *attitude is everything*. Thanks to my determined effort to build a more positive attitude, I had managed to get over my hurt and disappointment at not being drafted by the NBA. I'd put my positive attitude into action. Whether it was going to Alaska, meeting a person who questioned what I was doing with my life, Kenny's coaching me, or getting hired by IBM, it all came down to attitude.

Our Attitudes Affect Everything We Do

The next time you are faced with a difficult challenge, focus on staying positive. Remember that your setbacks can be setups for even greater opportunities. Tap into the power of a positive attitude and stay in the game by playing with your NBA: Natural-Born Abilities.

Optimists (individuals with positive attitudes) are more successful than similarly talented people with pessimistic or negative attitudes, according to Martin Seligman, a noted psychologist at the University of Pennsylvania. His research also indicates that negative attitudes can be changed to positive attitudes. Each of us can decide to change our primary attitude. Most people get health or dental checkups once or twice a year to maintain wellness. We also take our cars in for regular checkups to make sure that they keep running properly. Yet, sadly, we aren't nearly as careful about monitoring the attitudes that affect our mental health.

When was the last time you had an attitude tune-up? If you haven't been getting what you want out of life, if people are not responding well to you, could it be that you need one?

Seligman's study has shown that our attitudes—positive or negative—can affect whether we succeed or fail in reaching our goals. In his classic book, *Learned Optimism,* he offers empirical data showing that life insurance agents with optimistic attitudes sold more policies than did their pessimistic colleagues. Pessimists blamed failed sales attempts on themselves, which lowered their self-esteem and led to lower sales volumes. Optimists, rather than taking the rejections personally, had logical reasons to explain why prospects did not buy policies. Optimists not only sold 37 percent more than the pessimists did, they also remained on the job longer.

It is also true that those with positive attitudes generally enjoy better overall health. As positive thinking takes hold of your mind, your body responds accordingly. If you're having trouble accepting this concept, I'd like to make you blush. We blush when we're embarrassed, don't we? Isn't that physical reaction the result of a mere thought? We haven't actually exerted ourselves to make blood rush to our faces, causing them to redden. It's the thought that triggers this reaction. If we have this kind of physical reaction to a thought, is it such a leap of faith to believe that a positive thought could affect our bodies in a beneficial way?

Researchers have shown also that the simple act of smiling causes your brain to release a stream of chemicals that makes you feel good. The last few years have produced mounting research that positive thinking aids in the healing process. British researchers have gathered evidence showing a tie between negative emotions and illness.

The power of positive thinking has been documented scientifically in the real world of work and relationships. There are sound reasons for you to develop a process for maintaining a positive attitude. These are common-sense strategies that will help you develop your positive attitude. They work because as you eliminate stress and negative thinking, you'll begin to enjoy a more positive feeling about yourself, which is the first step in helping you turn attitude into action.

Your Attitude Reflects You

Although everyone has an attitude, not everyone has the same type of attitude. Some individuals' attitudes propel them along, helping them to deal with challenges, overcome obstacles, and accomplish their objectives. Others have attitudes that are anchors, slowing them down or stopping them altogether. Think about people you know who are often identified by their attitude:

He's got a can-do attitude.
That George, he's always on top of things.

> I don't know how Sarah does it; she can bring a
> smile to any situation.

The people described above are the sort of folks you like to be around, aren't they? You want to have them on your team at work and as your friends at home.

Then there are those people known for their negative attitudes:

> You know Ellen. If there's not a problem, she can
> create one.

> I know Hank is capable, but it's just too much
> work to get him to do anything.

> I had lunch with Fred. To hear him tell it, nothing
> good ever happens to him.

I'm sure you've met some of these individuals too. Because of their negative attitudes, they seem to carry dark clouds over their heads. We generally avoid interacting with them because of their negative approach to life.

Those with positive attitudes throw off the bed covers each morning, jump out of bed, throw open a window, take a deep breath, and say, "Good morning, God." Those with negative attitudes drag themselves out of bed, stare out the window, and say, "Good God, morning."

OK, it's not always that clear-cut. Even rabid optimists have bad days. Even the gloomiest pessimists have a good thought now and then. Often our attitudes are affected by the circumstances we deal with day to day. What happens *to* us influences what goes on *within* us unless we master a process for taking control of our attitudes to maintain a positive approach to life even when negative events occur.

George Bernard Shaw said, "People are always blaming their circumstances for what they are. The people who get on in this world are the people who get up and look for the circumstances they want and, if they can't find them, make them."

If you look around, you can find dozens of examples of people whose attitudes don't fit their apparent circumstances. One Sunday in church, I heard a beautiful soprano voice behind me. Her singing was so joyful that I had to see who it was. The voice belonged to a middle-aged lady sitting in a wheelchair. Her right arm was strapped to the chair. Her left hand rested on a little platform with a lever that controlled the chair. Someone had placed the hymnal in her lap so that she could read the verse and sing it. Evidently this woman had lost the use of all her limbs with the exception of the fingers of her left hand. Yet there was a smile on her face and, obviously, joy in her heart.

What happens to you does not have to live within you. Even bad circumstances can serve as stepping-stones to your goals. Every one of us endures hardships that can bring out the worst in us or inspire the best. It all comes down to which attitude you choose.

Attitudes at Work

Not long ago, I was having lunch in a restaurant staffed with a large contingent of twenty-something servers. The young man waiting on me was personable and took my order after a reasonable period of time, but I noticed that the young waitress serving a table close by was much more energetic and attentive. She had a bigger smile and a warmer disposition. What impressed me most was that when a party left one of her tables, she rushed over and cleared it. The other servers stood around talking while waiting for the harried buspeople to clean off the tables.

All of those employees were doing their jobs, but it seemed to me that this young woman was doing more. Her attitude was making a difference. Her customers appeared to be happier because they were seated more quickly. Her efficiency also benefited the restaurant's hosts since they could move people into tables more quickly. This waitress was not only making a difference for those around her, she was also making a tangible difference for herself. Her willingness to pitch in and clear her own tables meant that she was able to serve more customers and get more tips during the shift.

This may seem like a small thing, but I have developed a finely tuned antenna for attitudes over the years. I've seen many examples in which a positive attitude makes an enormous difference in career success. As a professional speaker and trainer, much of my work is done for major corporations. Managers invite me to speak to their sales forces, their office staffs, or their management groups. As a result, I get regular readings on the state of corporate America and working conditions in general.

In the last several years, I've detected a change that is reflected in the tone of the invitations I receive. It used to be that a corporate contact would call and say something like this: "Keith, we're going for a record year and I really want to keep my people pumped up. I'd like you to help us raise our attitudes another notch."

Today, the invitation is more likely to sound like this: "Keith, we've got a lot of challenges due to the merging of different cultures. Our people are more worried about their futures than their work. Frankly, I have to do something. What can you do to help?"

The workplace has changed dramatically. These days, companies are either downsizing, rightsizing, merging, or being acquired. Even white-collar professionals who thought their lives were secure through retirement are now feeling vulnerable—and with good reason. The world of work has become unstable. Experienced people are losing their jobs under rapidly shifting circumstances. Those who hold onto their jobs are dogged by concern that they might be next.

These are circumstances that can lead to negative attitudes and self-defeating actions if you allow the circumstances to dictate your life. Go into any corporation today, and you'll find people who are fearful of the future—and others who are excited by it. Their circumstances may well be the same. Each may be faced with unemployment, but some choose to see that as a dead end or defeat, while others choose to see it as an opportunity.

Consider the following situation involving Charley, who works in the computer industry. I'll let him lay it out for you:

I got fired from a job for having a bad attitude. My boss told me that I was doing pretty good work, but my negative attitude made it tough on him and everybody else in my department. I had a few weeks to think about it while I was looking for a job. My attitude had not helped me at all. I had done the work I was supposed to, and I had done it as well as anybody else. But instead of being recognized for doing good work, I got fired for having a bad attitude. It was pretty obvious that I needed to change my attitude.

In my next job, I promised myself that whatever happened, I would stay positive and do my job. I wasn't going to let my attitude get in the way of my job security and advancement. The second week I was there, they started downsizing. The only thing anybody talked about was who was going to be next. Maintaining a positive attitude was a little difficult. I sat down one night and wrote down these facts:

1. I have a job, and if I get fired, I'm no worse off than I was three weeks ago.
2. I'm learning some new skills, so I'm actually better off than I was three weeks ago.
3. If I work hard on my new skills, I'm going to be more valuable to this company or to some other company.
4. Sitting around stewing about it isn't going to help me, the company, or anybody else.

After that, my plan was obvious. I spent several evenings a week working on my programming skills. Every day, I went to work with a smile and did my job as well as I could. There was another round of downsizing. This time the president of the company lost his job too. The new president came in and made a speech about cutting expenses and moving the company to California. That led to more rumors and fears.

Before the move, I was offered a job with another company—with a 20 percent increase in pay. My evening studies paid off. The company I had worked for moved to California, but then they fired the new president. I don't know what they're going to do now, but I have a much better job.

This time, my attitude worked for me. With my old attitude, I would have been among the first to go, and I wouldn't have had a clue what to do about it. With my new attitude, I was able to deal with all the challenges. Controlling my attitude helped me keep the job I had and helped me get a better one. I'm a believer.

Dealing with negative attitudes in the workplace is one of the biggest challenges facing businesses, managers, and employees. A person with a negative attitude has the same power to influence others as a person with a positive attitude. The difference appears in the results. Positive attitudes in the workplace help improve communications and teamwork. Positive attitudes keep up morale and help increase productivity. The opposite can be said for negative attitudes. They dismantle teamwork, increase stress, and cripple productivity.

The difference between winners and losers in the workplace is often attitude. The salesperson who sells more, the manager who inspires her people, the manufacturing supervisor who commands respect and loyalty—all are beneficiaries of their positive attitudes. Many of my clients today are hiring for attitude and training for skills.

José Colmenares recruits employees for Southwest Airlines, the country's most acclaimed airline for the past decade. When hiring flight attendants, he doesn't look for a fixed set of skills or experiences, he told *Fast Company* magazine. He's searching instead for what the magazine described as "the perfect blend of energy, humor, team spirit, and self-confidence to match Southwest's famously offbeat and customer-obsessed culture."

Last year, Southwest, which has 22,000 employees, had openings for nearly 4,500 new people. It received more than 150,000 applications. Southwest's recruiters must identify the "elite few" who can make it at Southwest. What does Colmenares look for? A positive attitude!

Attitudes at Home

As a child, I don't remember wondering whether I would succeed or not. The only question was, what would I have to do to succeed? That's one of the most valuable gifts my parents gave me. Their examples helped me develop my own positive attitude toward life.

Some people seem to have the idea that since they have to be nice when they're out all day, they can be surly at home. A working mother comes home from her job and says she's tired of smiling. A working father vents all the frustrations he has collected during the day. They might argue that if you can't be yourself at home, where can you be?

I would argue this: If that's how you really are, then you need to start working on your attitude. A positive attitude is perhaps more important at home than anywhere else. As spouses and parents, one of our most vital roles is to help those we love feel good about themselves. If a father or mother carries around a negative attitude all day, it's extremely likely that the children in the house will come to blame themselves or adopt the same bad attitude.

I'll show you a little later how my mother's positive attitude helped me retain my self-confidence even when I had a potentially traumatic experience in kindergarten. Her ability to communicate her positive attitude helped me build my own foundation of self-confidence and optimism. We have a choice. We can concentrate on problems, or we can focus on solutions. I believe in taking the positive approach.

Your spouse may not understand you. Your children may not listen to you. Your parents may disagree with you. Those are all challenging circumstances, but they can be more effectively dealt with if you have a positive attitude. You will find that when your attitude improves, so do your circumstances.

Attitude into Action

Improving your attitude doesn't necessarily require making a 180-degree turn. Most of us are not 100 percent positive or negative all of the time. Even the most positive people have down time, and even the most negative people have a sunny day now and then. If you have trouble shaking the blues, though, you're headed for trouble unless you develop a process for adjusting your attitude. You can build a strong and powerful body with exercise, but it takes commitment and hard work. You have the same power to build a positive attitude with mental exercises. This too takes commitment, hard work, and continuous effort. Are you ready to get started on your attitude? Let's look at four things you must learn to do:

1. *Focus on handling stress.*

   The less stress you feel, the more energy you'll have to exercise those positive-thinking muscles. Though eliminating all stress from your life is an unrealistic goal, you can add to your energy levels by leading a more balanced life. If your work is stressful, look for ways to balance the time you spend at work with nonstressful leisure time. Some of us may need to devote a larger percentage of our time to work to keep that balance. The right balance hinges on your individual needs—don't try to fit into someone else's mold. Leisure time for one person could be reading a book or watching TV; for others it might be sewing, getting a manicure, fishing, building a cabinet, or jogging ten miles. The only thing that matters is that you choose what makes you feel relaxed and happy.

   If you're facing specific challenges—whether being a caregiver to an elderly parent, being a single parent, or simply feeling lonely—seek out support groups, or join a hobby club (photography, hiking) or a fitness center. Look for a group of people with whom you can connect and by whom you'll feel accepted and recognized.

2. *Identify your negative/pessimistic thoughts.*

I'll never be able to finish this project. I'm not good enough to apply for this promotion. The moment you catch yourself thinking those pessimistic thoughts, counter them with facts: *Time is limited. I need help with copying and collating. Jeannie will help if I ask. If we get behind, I'll ask Mr. Jones if we can get more help. . . . They want five years of management experience and I only have three and a half. I have more computer knowledge and education than what they're asking. I'm going to give it a shot.*

Don't let up on defeating those negative thoughts. The more you fight them with facts and rational thinking, the more positive muscle you're building. You want this process to become automatic. (We'll talk more about this in Chapter 3.)

3. *Tell a supportive person how you feel.*

Feelings left bottled up fester. You may also be isolating yourself, and many studies show that social isolation is a significant risk to your health. If you want to apply for that position but can't shake those self-doubts, share them with a trusted friend. The support and encouragement you get will give you added ammunition against negative thinking.

4. *Act to settle a problem.*

If you're stressed by a conflict with a co-worker, deal with the situation directly: "I know we disagree on how to implement this project. Would you be willing to work it out with me?" Or if a friend says or does something that hurts your feelings, tell him or her.

Attitude affects everything you do, both personally and professionally. Embrace your next attitude tune-up with a little checking and testing. Remember, your attitude reflects you. Resolving a problem will relieve your stress more quickly and effectively than just complaining about it. Even if you don't actually reach a solution, moving toward a solution is still less stressful than trying to ignore it.

Attitude Tune-Up

- What is your personal definition of *attitude*?
- What is your attitude toward life?
- Regardless of life's ups and downs, play with your (NBA) Natural-Born Abilities.
- How does your attitude reflect you? Are you a *Good Morning, God!* person more often than *Good God, morning!* person?
- Do you positively affect the lives of those with whom you interact?
- Think of the individuals in your life that affect you in a positive way and those who affect you in a negative way.
- When was the last time your attitude made a difference, bad or good?

No matter what you do in life, if you have a positive attitude, you'll always be 100 percent. According to our alphabet system, if you assign a numerical value to each letter (1–26), attitude will equal 100 percent.

$$
\begin{array}{rcl}
A & = & 1 \\
T & = & 20 \\
T & = & 20 \\
I & = & 9 \\
T & = & 20 \\
U & = & 21 \\
D & = & 4 \\
E & = & 5 \\
\hline
\text{ATTITUDE} & = & 100
\end{array}
$$

CHAPTER TWO

Attitude Is a Choice

STEP 2
Choose to take charge of your life.

This step helps you recognize how your choices today impact your success tomorrow. Taking charge and staying in control is an attitude of choice. It's your next step for turning attitude into action.

I woke up and realized I was running late. I had to get to the airport to catch a flight. I drove seventy-five to eighty miles per hour to Hartsfield International. I ran up to the ticket counter and told the clerk I was running late: "Quick, I've got to catch the plane to San Francisco. Tell me the gate number."

"You're going out of Concourse D. You've only got fifteen minutes," he said. "I don't think you're going to make it."

I'm not going to make it talking to you, so would you please give me my ticket!

I had a choice about how I would react to this situation. We all have a choice about how we react to each and every situation in our lives. Sometimes people tell you what you can't do because they don't see themselves achieving it. But the magic of the word *triumph* is in the first syllable. You've got to *try*.

I snatched that ticket and started running. I got through security. In the Atlanta airport, there's a train you have to catch to get to the concourse. I was running so fast I didn't have to catch the train.

I wasn't just running, I was talking to myself too. *Come on, you've got to go. You can't miss this flight. You've got to get there.* I was moving. I hit the escalator and never stopped running. My inner voice said, *Boy, you're out of shape. You'd better start working out.*

When I finally approached the gate, I noticed that the plane was still there. An airline agent was at the gate.

"Excuse me, ma'am," I said. "I ran all the way from the ticket counter. Did I make it?"

"We just got a phone call, the plane's going to be two hours delayed."

I looked at her and I said, "That's OK. I'm positive and proactive." She said, "I don't care what you call yourself. We're not leaving for two hours."

As I started to walk away, I saw another gentleman come up behind me and approach the counter. He appeared to be a top-level executive. He said, "Excuse me, ma'am, is the flight leaving on time?" She told him they were having mechanical difficulties and that the flight would be leaving in two hours.

He became angry. "Mechanical difficulties! Do you know who you're talking to? I'm a million miler, flying colonel. I know the CEO personally. I want to speak to your supervisor right now."

A supervisor in a nice red jacket appeared. This guy argued with her for thirty-five minutes.

Can you guess what time the plane left?

Two hours later.

I guarantee you, nobody wanted to sit next to him.

This fellow had another choice. He could have accepted the delay and made constructive use of his time.

The difference in our attitudes that day made the difference in our behaviors. I don't know that the executive suffered any serious consequences as a result of his anger, but I do know that he didn't accomplish anything positive, because he let his circumstances control his attitude.

I thought about the positive things that I could do. How could I reframe this situation? I went and got something to eat—a grilled chicken sandwich and a large orange juice. I went to the bookstore and bought a book, Norman Vincent Peale's *Enthusiasm Makes a Difference*. Read chapter one right in the airport. Then I did something special. I believe that any time you're going through something, you've always got to go inward to find out what little things you can do to bring joy to your life. I love popcorn. If you ever see me in an airport, you'll always find me looking for the popcorn. If you're ever in Atlanta, Concourse D, it's gate 19, $1.58 a box. I went and bought a box of popcorn.

Then I did something extra special. I called my grandma. Any time I'm going through something and I need a pick-me-up, all I've got to do is call Grandma. She lives in Seattle. After a fifteen-minute conversation with my grandma, I forgot all about the flight being late. It didn't even matter.

If you can visualize me going back to the gate, I'm smiling and whistling. I've had something to eat, read chapter one of a great book, had some popcorn, and talked to my grandma. When I returned to the gate, I looked at the passengers waiting for the flight, and some of them looked extremely toxic. I truly believe that toxic attitudes rub off, and exposure to them, over a period of time, might damage my attitude.

I scanned the area, chose a seat, and sat down next to a gentleman. I was just sitting there eating my popcorn, minding my own business. The man sitting next to me looked at me and asked, "Why are you so happy? Don't you know we've been here for an hour and a half? We've got another thirty minutes to go."

I responded, "I have a choice and I'm choosing to be positive."

He said, "Positive about what?"

I looked at him and stated, "Let me give you three reasons. This flight is delayed either because there is something wrong with the plane, something wrong with the weather, or something wrong with the pilot. In case any of those three scenarios are true, I'm happy to be sitting here talking to you. I'd rather be here wishing I was up there than to be up there wishing I was here."

He looked at me, smiled, and said, "You've got a point. So how about sharing some of that popcorn?"

The Power of Choice

What is it going to be for you: a positive attitude or a negative attitude? The choice seems fairly simple, doesn't it? The problem is that we often forget we have a choice. That is one of the master keys to unlocking your greatness in life—exercising your power to choose your attitude and your approach to life's challenges. We make choices consciously and unconsciously all of our lives. We choose when to get out of bed, what to wear, what to eat, where to go, and when to come home. Most of the simple decisions we make unconsciously. You should choose your attitude thoughtfully because it determines how you respond to the many challenges you will encounter.

A good friend of mine is basically in the place he was fifteen years ago. He hasn't had much success. I talked to him about his failure to achieve the goals he'd set. He identified what it was that had held him back. "Bad choices," he said, "and not making any choice at all."

Sometimes making no choice is the worst decision of all. It's vital that you consciously choose the right attitude and that you choose it wisely. The paths our lives take are largely determined by the choices we make day in and day out. A friend related the following story about the power of choice in her life:

I was three years old, but I still remember the day. We were on a family vacation. My parents and an uncle had rented a cabin on a lake. It was a beautiful summer day. The sun was out and everything was in full bloom. I remember being in the boat, on the lake, laughing and playing. I didn't see the accident, or remember much about the rest of the day. I just know that on that day, I lost my father.

My mother never seemed to recover from the loss. She began drinking to ease the pain. It didn't help. When I was nine years old, my two older sisters and I were taken from my mother and placed in foster care. For several years, we moved from home to home. Some were abusive. We stayed in foster care until an older cousin took us in. At first it was very difficult. My cousin's wife made it very clear that she had not wanted the responsibility of raising us. Eventually my two sisters moved back to our hometown. I remained in the care of my cousin. My cousin's love helped me overcome my fears and disappointments.

I didn't make all the right choices. I married at the age of twenty. I had a baby girl at twenty-three, and I was divorced by the age of twenty-five. Three years later, I lost my aunt to breast cancer. She'd been the only real mother I'd had. Her last words were to tell me how much she loved me. Again my choices were not good. I became a heavy drinker. It took me a year before I realized that I had made the same choice as my mother. I didn't like who I was becoming. I decided I had a choice. I immediately went into rehab.

It's been thirteen years. I have never once looked back. My daughter is a beautiful young woman now. I remarried. I now have an eight-year-old son and two beautiful bonus gifts, my second husband's children. I have been with the same company for twenty-two years, and I've gone back to school to obtain my bachelor's degree. I have a year to go to graduation.

My cousin taught me how to overcome obstacles, and he also showed me the true meaning of love. It's all about attitude and the power of choice. I learned that I had control of my destination by the choices I made. I know that there will always be obstacles in life's journey. I just choose to see them as challenges to overcome. What a joy!

Choice is the starting point to everything we do in life. The legendary Harvard psychologist and philosopher William James said that one of the most important discoveries made by his generation was that by changing our attitudes, we can change our lives. It's a choice we all have.

Bitter or Better? It's Your Choice!

I'm sure you notice that some people seem to have an unshakable self-confidence while others never seem to believe in themselves. The self-confident people may suffer setbacks, make mistakes, or get dragged down by hard times, but they still believe they will weather the storm and come out on top. Those who don't believe in themselves never seem to find their way. Often they just seem to drift with the tides.

A man came up to me after attending one of my seminars and said, "I know attitude is important, but it's not as simple as that for me. There's nothing I can do to improve mine." I'm afraid this gentleman has forgotten one of the most basic but crucial differences between himself and a potted palm. He has the power to make choices. He can choose to wallow in a cold puddle of self-pity or he can step out into the warm light. It's a choice. There is always a choice.

The critical difference between those who believe that they will succeed and those who have no belief in themselves is their understanding of attitude. There are those who know they can control their attitudes and those who allow their attitudes to control them. The people who do best in life are those who realize they have the power to choose their attitudes, just as they have the power to choose their clothing, their cars, or their dinner companions.

CONTROLLED BY ATTITUDE

People in this category lack faith in their ability to overcome difficulties and don't understand their own power. When they are hit by hard times, they go down. They stay there until they've been down so long it looks like up to them. Many never get up at all. People who are controlled by attitude tend to believe not only that they can't control their lives but that life has it in for them. They are pessimists by nature.

When something bad happens to them—and bad things happen to everyone—their tendency is to believe that the difficulties will last a long time, eventually wiping them out. They also tend to perceive challenging times as special punishments dished out only to them because of past sins. They have a very fatalistic approach to life. They see even the good times and life's blessings as merely a setup for bad things to come. For them, all defeats are permanent, all mistakes are fatal, all missed opportunities are gone forever. When faced with a challenge, they often talk of being overwhelmed by the enormity of it. They exaggerate the size of the problem and put down their ability to respond. *This is the absolute worst thing that has ever happened to me. I'll never have the resources to deal with it.*

ATTITUDE UNDER CONTROL

These folks know that though they may not be able to control their circumstances, they can control how they respond to them. They are optimistic by nature, and even when life hits them hard, they see setbacks as temporary interruptions caused by circumstances they cannot control. When faced with challenges, they tend to focus on the solution rather than the problem.

Change Your Focus, Change Your Attitude

As the winner of the world and U.S. pro cycling championships, Lance Armstrong was a twenty-five-year-old rising star on the international circuit. Then, in 1996, he discovered that a particularly deadly form of cancer had spread from his testicles to his stomach, lungs, and brain. Doctors said he had only a 50 percent chance of surviving. His racing career was put on hold for more than a year while he underwent intensive chemotherapy.

Someone who felt helpless about controlling his attitude probably would have plunged into depression or despair and given up. But Lance Armstrong amazed his doctors and much of the world by not letting his extreme circumstances defeat him. Instead, he got back on his bicycle and continued to train during his treatments, sometimes riding as much as fifty miles a day.

Although others might have chosen an attitude of helplessness, despair, or defeat, Lance Armstrong chose a combative attitude toward the disease that threatened his life. It's true that many people have fought cancer bravely and still lost out in spite of courageous efforts. But for reasons that even his doctors have not yet determined, Armstrong won. His cancer disappeared entirely.

Since this is real life and not a made-for-TV movie, Lance Armstrong still had challenges to deal with. The life-threatening experience drained him emotionally and spiritually. For a brief period the cyclist went into a depression. He refused even to get on his racing bike. He spent several weeks acting like a reckless kid instead of a serious athlete, but as the time approached for a charity race he had committed to, Armstrong once again asserted his power to choose his attitude and his response to challenging times.

With the encouragement of close friends, he began riding again to rebuild his strength and to rediscover his love of competitive cycling. He chose an attitude of gratitude for being given another chance at life. As a result, he reached new levels of accomplishment, which are every bit as astounding as his defeat of cancer. In the summer of 1999, he set a new world record in winning one of the sports world's most demanding events, the 2,285-mile Tour de France.

The power to choose is one of the greatest gifts God has given us. Armstrong chose an attitude that empowered him. He battled briefly with a more negative attitude, but to be fair, he had been through one of life's most difficult tests and he was exhausted physically and mentally. In the end, the most important thing is that he realized he had the power to choose another, more constructive attitude, and he did.

Happiness Is Yours to Create

We all want to be happy and fulfilled. Often, though, we demand too much of life. We set strict criteria for what will make us happy. When those criteria are not met, we develop attitudes that only make matters worse. The most basic, most revealing question you can ask yourself is, *What does it take to make me happy?*

- Do you have to be happy every minute of every day?
- Does everyone have to do what you want them to do?
- Does every aspect of your work have to be fulfilling all the time?
- Do you have to be making more money than everyone else?
- Do you have to have more power than everyone else?
- Do you have to be recognized and rewarded for everything you do?
- Do you have to be loved by everyone you know?

The same attitude spoils many relationships. I've seen many of them fail because one or both of the people involved demanded too much of the other. Not everyone is perfectly neat, beautiful, charming, loving, funny, or attentive all the time. Life isn't a romance novel. Barbie and Ken are plastic. Even Richard Gere and Cindy Crawford discovered that beauty, money, fame, and charm don't guarantee a perfect relationship.

We often demand too much of love and friendship, and the same is true of happiness. It's easy to be happy if you can find happiness in small doses. If you set impossible criteria for happiness, then it will be all but impossible for you to be happy.

Build Your Attitude from the Inside Out

For true happiness, it's best to look within yourself rather than rely on others or the world around you. The sad but true fact is that it's difficult to be happy if you rely on outside sources. The root of happiness is joy, and joy lives within you. It's not influenced by external events.

Melissa was in the retail clothing business. She was always in a good mood. She always had something positive to say. She was a unique manager because she inspired her employees and everyone who came into the store. She never had a bad day or a down moment. Melissa would always tell her employees to look on the positive side of every situation.

Every time I went into the store I noticed Melissa's upbeat, enthusiastic attitude. Irate customers didn't seem to affect her. She had smiles and kind words for everyone. So one day I went up to Melissa and said, "I don't get it. You can't be a positive person all the time. How do you do it?"

"Each morning I wake up and say to myself, 'Melissa you have two choices. You can choose to be in a good mood, or you can choose to be in a bad mood.' I choose to be in a good mood. Each time something happens, I can choose to be a victim or I can choose to learn from it. I choose to learn from it. Every time someone comes to me complaining, I can choose to accept their complaining or I can point out the positive side of life. I point out the positive side of life."

"It can't be that easy," I protested.

"Yes, it is," Melissa said. "Life is all about choices. When you cut away all the junk, every situation is a choice. You choose how you react to situations. You choose how people will affect your mood. You choose to be in a good mood or a bad mood. The bottom line: It's your choice how you live."

Several months after that conversation, I was in the mall and stopped by the store just to say hello to Melissa. She wasn't there. One of the employees informed me that she had been in a near-fatal automobile accident. She had suffered internal bleeding, a punctured lung, a broken collarbone, and a broken leg.

After twelve hours of surgery, weeks of intensive care, and months of physical therapy, Melissa was back at work. I saw her shortly after she returned and asked her how she was doing after such a challenging time.

"I feel super-fantastic," she said.

When I asked her what she remembered about the accident, Melissa replied, "I'm sure glad I had my seat belt on. I remembered that I had two choices: I could choose to live or I could choose to die. I chose to live."

"Did you lose consciousness?" I asked.

"No, but the paramedics had a great attitude," she said. "They kept telling me I was going to be fine. But when they wheeled me into the emergency room, I saw the expressions on the faces of the doctors and nurses and got really scared.

In their eyes I read, 'I don't think she's going to survive.' I took an attitude that I had a choice and I was going to live."

Melissa lived not only because of the skill of her doctors but also because of her faith and positive attitude. Melissa's story proves that every day we have a choice about how we're going to live our lives.

Your Choices Determine Your Happiness

The quality of our lives is determined by the choices we make: which career path we take, which partner we choose, the lifestyle we embrace. I learned my first lesson in the power of choosing attitude on my first day of school. It may seem strange, considering that I make my living as a professional speaker, but I was a stutterer for most of my childhood. Until I reached school age, it was never made to seem like a problem. I was always assured that I would grow out of it. I had an uncle who'd stuttered as a child, lost it as an adolescent, and become a respected college professor. My mother and grandmother always reminded me of that, and they'd tell me that I stuttered only because "your brain is working faster than your mouth."

I didn't think of it as a negative thing until my first day of kindergarten. I was five years old. I was so excited to be around the other kids and to find a desk in the front row with my name on it. My teacher, Miss Peterson, was a very positive, dynamic woman who glowed with energy and enthusiasm. She told us right off that she thought we were going to be the best class in the school. Then she started to go around the room asking us to say our names so everyone could get to know each other. She asked me to go first. I jumped up, turned and faced my new classmates, and started stuttering terribly because I was so excited. *My, my, mymymymm . . .*

I'll never forget the girl with pigtails in the back of the room. Her name was Nancy. She jumped up and said, "He can't talk. He stutters." Everyone laughed at that. Then the boy next to me, Billy, who later became my best friend, looked at me and said, "You're too tall. You shouldn't be in our room." The kids all giggled at that too. Miss Peterson must have said something to the class, but I was so wrapped up in what the kids said that I didn't notice.

It's the Internal Messages That Count

I was hurt, of course. I wanted my mom. I had never felt that kind of pain. I kept repeating those negative comments. *You're too tall. You can't talk. You shouldn't be here.* That feeling of not belonging is a terrible one whether you are a kid in kindergarten or an adult in a corporate office. Do you remember the book *All I Really Need to Know I Learned in Kindergarten*? That's me. I learned about rejection. I learned that people can say things that hurt you. And, thanks to my mother, I learned that you can choose not to be hurt or rejected.

The voices of my classmates had grown louder and louder inside my head. Later in life, I learned that the strongest and most destructive voice is your own. It was sure true in this instance. While the teacher and my classmates went on about the first day of school, I sat there talking to myself and telling myself that I didn't belong in school. *I'm too tall. I can't talk. I want to go home.* I laid low until our first recess. Then I bolted.

I ran home. We lived about two miles away. I took one breath the whole way. Set the world speed record from kindergarten to front porch on the first day of school. As fast as I ran, Miss Peterson was faster. My mom was hanging up the phone when I hit the porch. I ran into her arms, and she gave me a world-class hug. It was the hug of a lifetime. I can still feel that hug.

I remember looking up at my mom and saying, "I'm too tall. I can't talk. I don't fit."

"Miss Peterson told me what happened," she said. "There is good news."

Good news? I stopped crying at that. What good news could there be? No more kindergarten? Home schooling with Miss Peterson?

"The good news is that you tried. I'm proud of you for that. My little man tried, and even though you are not able to say your name as well as you would like, that's OK. This is going to be a challenge, but I'm convinced that if we work hard, one day, and I do mean one day, all the kids will listen when you say your name loud and clear. Son, don't ever forget that you are special."

My mom effectively replaced the negative messages I'd heard from my classmates with a far more positive message. When I ran away from school, it was because my inner voice had been repeating their words: *You're too tall. You talk funny. You don't belong.* I went back to school with my mom's words on my inner tape recorder: *I'm not different, I'm special. I can learn to talk without a stutter, and then they will understand.*

Suddenly I wasn't speech-impaired. I was working on a challenge. Again, the reality had not changed. I still stuttered, but my perception of my speech impediment had changed. Another paradigm shifted, a new attitude created. And that attitude changed everything. It was my weapon against the teasing and the mocking.

My mother taught me then and there that *attitude is a choice.* When I told her I couldn't go back to school, she listened and understood what was contributing to that negative attitude.

She was able to listen to the pain that fueled my fears and humiliation. She then gave me that opportunity to choose a new attitude: "Honey, you've got a choice. You can accept an attitude of humiliation and fear, or you can take on an attitude of action. You can be a victim or a victor. You can let life run you over, or you can take it on! You have a choice!"

My mom showed me a way out of fear and humiliation. That's when we went back and got very clear on some things that we had to do. She gave me insight and inspiration. She showed me that even as a small, insecure boy, I had the power to choose a better way.

A Positive Attitude Is the First and Last Line of Defense

I'm not going to tell you that I didn't have setbacks from time to time. It was tough being a stutterer. Kids can be relentless in mocking and teasing you. In bed at night, I'd talk to God and ask him why he made me stutter. It affected nearly every aspect of my life, and maintaining a positive attitude was a huge challenge.

I took speech lessons for six years and used to lie about why I was getting out of regular class to go somewhere else. The teachers in elementary school kept paper clocks on the blackboard for students who had "special needs." When I had to go to speech class, I was supposed to go to the front of the class, take the paper clock off the blackboard, and go out the back door quietly. It was not possible for me to slip out unnoticed. I was always the tallest person in my class. Many teachers even looked up to me. Some kid would always see me get up and start mocking me: "I'm-m-m g-g-g-going t-t-t-to. . . ."

Most of the time, I tuned them out and focused on getting better. By fifth grade, I was determined to beat my stuttering. I always hated being called on to read aloud, but when my turn came, I was determined to get through my assigned paragraphs. The other kids always hoped I'd get picked first. They knew that once I got up, no one else would have to read. I'd struggle with a paragraph for twenty minutes. By the time I got through my section, it was time for math!

I had my days of attitudinal backsliding. Anger, rejection, or embarrassment sometimes ruled the day. But I never forgot the lesson communicated in my mother's hug and her words of encouragement: *You are special. You can choose not to be hurt or discouraged. You can choose a positive attitude over a negative attitude. And you can overcome this challenge.*

Selecting an Optimistic Attitude

Growing up in Seattle, I knew a set of identical twins named Seymour and Fillmore. (OK, so I'm making this up as I go along, bear with me.) Seymour was a natural-born optimist. Every night he went to bed with these words: "I can't wait until tomorrow 'cause I get better looking every day!"

Fillmore was a Sad Sack by comparison. He always looked for the black cloud over the silver lining. He even considered his name to be an indication that he'd been born half-empty.

Since the boys were supposed to be identical twins, their parents grew worried at the disparity in their personalities and took them to a psychologist. He suggested that the parents work at balancing out the twins' divergent personalities at their next co-birthday party: "Put them in separate rooms to open their gifts. Give Fillmore the best gift you can afford, and give Seymour a box of horse manure," advised the psychologist.

The parents followed his instructions and carefully observed the results. When they looked in on Fillmore, they heard his usual griping, even though they'd given him a state-of-the-art computer. "I wanted an iMac, not a Compaq," he complained.

Next they peeked through the door of Seymour's room, holding their noses at the stink of his gift. To their amazement, he was merrily digging through the box of manure with his hands and crying out joyfully, "This is incredible! I know there's got to be a pony in here somewhere!"

That's the power of a positive attitude!

"Life inflicts the same setbacks and tragedies on the optimist as on the pessimist, but the optimist weathers them better," writes psychologist Martin Seligman. "As we have seen the optimist bounces back from defeat, and, with his life somewhat poorer, he picks up and starts again. The pessimist gives up and falls into depression."

Dr. Seligman's research also found that your attitude can be consciously changed from negative to positive by learning how to coach your inner dialogue. "Becoming an optimist consists . . . of learning a set of skills about how to talk to yourself when you suffer a personal defeat," he notes.

We have a choice. We can choose an inner dialogue of self-encouragement and self-motivation, or we can choose one of self-defeat and self-pity. It's a power we all have. Each of us encounters hard times, hurt feelings, heartache, and physical and emotional pain. The key is to realize it's not what happens to you that matters, it's how you choose to respond.

Programming Your Attitude

Think of your mind as a computer that can be programmed. You can choose whether the software that is installed is productive or unproductive. Your inner dialogue is the software that programs your attitude, which determines how you present yourself to the world around you. You have control over what that programming is. Whatever you put into it is reflected in what comes out.

Hundreds of different situations program our attitude each day, and most of them have the potential to be positive or negative. The subconscious mind never sleeps. You can't pull a fast one on the subconscious. Whatever it has heard—from others, and especially from your own inner dialogue—it records . . . and keeps.

Most people allow their brains to be programmed indiscriminately. The computer adage "Garbage in, garbage out," as it applies to our own very personal computer—the brain—should be stated as "Garbage in, garbage stays." The brain hears negative things and accepts them as truth. Many of us have behavior patterns today that were programmed into our brains at a very tender age. The information that was recorded by our brains could have been completely inaccurate or even cruel.

Think of a sunflower seed you plant and nurture. That seed was programmed by nature to be a sunflower. Don't even think about trying to make it into a pumpkin or a rose. It was programmed to be a sunflower, and that's the end of it. Some of us were programmed at a very early age to behave a certain way. Maybe part of your programming tells you that you're not very smart, and you believe it and your actions bear it out. You might have a learning disorder, but maybe you simply have faulty programming. After all, there are many people with serious learning disorders who were programmed by loving parents and caring teachers to believe they could overcome their barriers . . . and they did.

The Power of Positive Inner Dialogue

The key to ridding yourself of this attitude of helplessness is to clear your mind of negative inner conversations and replace them with more hopeful messages. You can reframe your perspective by changing and controlling your inner dialogue. The longer negative thoughts are allowed to churn in your mind, the greater the emotional buildup and the potential damage. If you don't recognize and treat it, you could face the psychological equivalent of pneumonia—depression.

We like to think that our attitudes are affected by what people do and say to us, but in reality, it is what we say to *ourselves* that has the greatest influence on how we present ourselves to the world. When the kids in my class made fun of me on my first day of kindergarten, their words hit me and hurt. By accepting what they said and replaying it over and over in my head, I convinced myself that I didn't belong. At the first opportunity, I fled home. My mother then wisely reconstructed my inner conversation by giving me positive words and thoughts to replace the negative.

Watch What You Say—To Yourself

The loudest and most influential voice you hear is your own inner voice, your "self-critic." It can work for you or against you, depending on the messages you allow. It can be pessimistic or optimistic. It can wear you down or cheer you on. You control the sender and the receiver, but only if you consciously take responsibility and control of your inner conversation.

I first began tapping into the power of positive inner conversations as a kid practicing basketball. I'd pretend I was one of my basketball heroes—Jamaal Wilkes, an NBA All-Star with the Los Angeles Lakers. Wilkes was known as Silk because he was such a smooth, controlled player. He never lost his temper. He was never angered. That's how I wanted to play, so I started an inner dialogue while I was practicing or playing. *You're smooth as silk,* I'd tell myself. It was a way of asserting emotional control. If a guy elbowed me or shoved me, I'd turn it up: *Smooth as silk, nothing throws me off my game!*

That inner dialogue turned out to be pretty powerful. I started calling myself Smooth as Silk, or Silk for short, to embed it deeper into my subconscious, and pretty soon my teammates, the fans, and sportswriters picked up on it too. Even now, my mother still has license plates that say SILK.

By keeping that inner dialogue going during games, I controlled my emotions on the court. I held my temper. I didn't get overly excited or agitated. I kept control of my attitude, and that sense of control gave me greater self-confidence. One of my greatest memories of playing in high school was a semifinal game in the state tournament. My Garfield High School team had a 22–0 record of wins to losses, and on the day of this game, the *Seattle Times* ran a story saying we were one of the best teams in the state's history. That was a big reputation to carry into the game against a very strong team from Tacoma's Lincoln High School.

They had prepared well for us. They broke our press, played strong defense, and did a good job of executing their offense. We were playing catch-up for most of the game, and with just three minutes left we were down by seven points.

During a time-out, I could tell that my teammates were frustrated and close to giving up. We had let all the good publicity and our undefeated record go to our heads. We'd forgotten that we had to earn it. There were a lot of negative comments in the huddle, and finally I'd had enough. "We are going to win this game," I told my teammates. "Give me the ball."

Yes, it was a Hollywood moment. A West Coast version of Hoosiers. We won by seven points, and I learned another lesson in the power of attitude. The fact that I said out loud that we were going to win the game changed the perspective of my teammates. They had lost confidence, but when I showed them that I had not lost mine, they got back in the game.

When we control our decisions, we control our actions; a positive attitude helps produce a positive action. Here's an example.

Through a friend of a friend, and at a rather steep price, I got tickets—fourth row center—to an NBA playoff game. A man approached and loomed over me, saying, "Haul it out of here, pal. These are my seats!" My first reaction was to yell back, "Take a hike!" Instead I stopped to think: "No way am I giving up these seats. But if it gets ugly, we could both be thrown out of the arena."

So with a concerned look on my face I said, "Maybe I read my tickets wrong." I pulled out my tickets and placed them next to his so we could compare. His tickets were for seats 6 and 8, row 4, section 101—the section directly opposite mine. "Well, I do have your seat numbers all right, but you're in section 101, on the other side of the court. Looks like we both have the best seats in the house." The man was relieved. He smiled, mumbled an apology, and happily rushed off to the right section.

The experience could have been a complete disaster if I had acted on my initial thought. I had a choice. By choosing to control my thoughts and maintaining a positive attitude, I allowed us all to enjoy a great basketball game. Whether someone approaches you in a negative, combative manner or whether you need to make the first move in a situation, the ball is in your court. If you set a positive tone, the chances of a positive outcome are very good.

We often have to fight for control over our professional and personal lives. Someone or something always seems to be fighting us for control. Every day we meet individuals who need to control those around them; sometimes we have that same need. Fortunately, we each have the ability to control our own lives. How we choose to use that control can alter our life's direction for the bad or for the good.

Attitude Tune-Up

- What positive choices are you going to make to help put your attitude into action?
- Are you a controlled-by-attitude or an attitude-under-control person?
- The root of your happiness is your joy. Don't let anybody steal your joy.
- Program your attitude with positive internal dialogue. Remember: Garbage in, garbage stays.

The greatest power that a person possesses is the power to choose.

—J. MARTIN KOHE

CHAPTER THREE

Bag Your Bad Attitude

STEP 3
*Identify through self-awareness
the attitudes that hold you back
or propel you forward.*

In this step you will learn how to transform turning
points into learning points to help turn your attitude into action.

I saw the negative effects of a bad attitude during my first
year on the Seattle University basketball team. Our coach
was a great recruiter and, during the off-season, a personable
guy. Yet he developed a negative attitude during our first season together, and it took a toll on all of us. I decided to play
for Seattle University's Chieftains instead of the more celebrated University of Washington team because he totally
charmed me. He pushed all my buttons. When he came to
visit me during my high school career, this coach told me I'd
be one of the focal points of his team's offense, which would
then help me get the attention of NBA scouts.

He was a great recruiter, but once practice started, he turned negative. He criticized us and wore us down mentally and physically. Too often he focused on what we did wrong instead of what we needed to do to become better. He'd tell me that I wasn't getting enough rebounds, but he never offered suggestions for how I might get more.

In fairness, I think Coach was stressed out because we were in a rebuilding season. We'd lost two great players the year before, and we were inexperienced. We probably lacked a lot of the skills and mental toughness he believed were necessary to win. Still, he had a negative attitude. Instead of constantly comparing us to the team he had before, why not look at us as the team we could become? We were a different group of players, but we still had skills. If he had made the adjustment, I think we all would have benefited. The older players might have responded better to his tough-love approach. But since we younger ones hadn't developed our confidence to that level, we needed a more positive approach. We needed to hear that our coach believed in us.

I will never forget my first day of fall basketball practice. I was taking my man one-on-one, setting him up for a move I had worked on all summer, when I heard Coach yell at the top of his voice, "Pass the ball. You're taking too long. You'll probably miss that shot anyway."

I'd been playing well over the summer. I had visions of greatness. But by the opening game I had lost my confidence. My attitude was in a tailspin. I'd become afraid to shoot for fear of being criticized from the bench.

Looking back, it wasn't entirely the coach's fault that I allowed his negative comments to impact my performance. I didn't know anything about monitoring my inner dialogue to fight off a negative attitude. Later in life I realized that you don't have to let what someone else says affect you negatively. You can hear the words, but you can choose your attitude. In those days, my self-image and my attitude were very dependent on what my coach said. And he wasn't inclined to waste his voice on encouraging words.

After one especially bad game, he kept repeating my miserable stats over and over in front of my teammates, questioning how I'd ever been named a high school All-American. I had played poorly, I admit. You hear about a player being "in the zone." I was in the *Twilight Zone*. It's a wonder I didn't shrink down to five-feet-six in that first season. I kept my height, but I lost all confidence. Long after my playing days were over, I'd still wake up wondering why I passed up so many shots that first year. I was afraid to make a mistake.

To make matters worse, the following year I got sick. I had to sit out my sophomore season because of pneumonia and pleurisy, a weakening of the lungs. Since he didn't have me to kick around anymore, Coach rode the rest of the team so hard that they threatened to mutiny. I'd been named team captain at the start of our sophomore year, so the guys came to me and asked me to talk to him and get him to ease up. When I went to tell him their concerns, this is what he said: "I'm thirty-five years old. This is how I coach. I'm too old to change. I'll just have to put together a whole new team next year if everyone on this team leaves."

Two years later, the coach was gone.

Some people get downsized or rightsized. He got attitude-sized. He had no one to blame but himself. The attitude alarms were going off all around him, but he wouldn't listen. His players were telling him. His assistant coaches were telling him. I told him. He ignored us all. He refused to acknowledge that his attitude was way out of whack. And it cost him his job.

Bad Attitudes Are Heavy Baggage

Maybe he was under a lot of stress. Maybe he was underpaid by the university or underappreciated by his team. Maybe his father or his coaches had used negative feedback as a motivational tool, and it worked for him. I could never understand why he had such a poor attitude. It didn't help him. It didn't help his players either.

It's not always easy to determine why other people have bad attitudes, but it's certainly easy to pick them out of a crowd. You could probably name a half-dozen co-workers, relatives, or others you know with bad attitudes. It's relatively easy to spot someone with a bad attitude. Unless, of course, that someone is you. If you haven't been getting what you want out of life, if you feel stuck, overlooked, unappreciated, or unfulfilled, it could be that you've picked up an attitude that is holding you back.

You might not see it in yourself, but you may have noticed that the people around you respond differently to you. If your relationships with bosses, co-workers, or employees have changed for the worse, if your loved ones or friends don't treat you the same way, maybe it's not them. Maybe it's you!

A Good Attitude Begins with Self-Awareness

The ability to recognize our feelings as they come over us is called self-awareness, and it is critical to our development in a highly mobile, fast-changing, and complex society. Self-awareness allows you to be aware of your emotions and attitudes. Knowing yourself and understanding what drives your attitude and emotions is the first step to self-knowledge and self-control. If you remember the experiences that trigger a bad or self-destructive attitude, you can then work to disarm those triggers and even replace the bad emotions with more constructive and empowering emotions to create a better attitude.

Self-awareness is very important. When you tell yourself *I shouldn't be thinking about this before I go to sleep,* you are practicing self-awareness because you are monitoring your emotions and judging their potential impact.

When you practice self-awareness, you give yourself far greater control of your actions. This control gives you options. You can decide not to react to negative emotions. Instead you can develop a positive attitude that allows you to let go of the emotion. You can also channel the energy of the negative emotion into a positive action.

If you don't learn to control or rechannel a negative attitude, it can have a terrible impact on your life. It may have already happened. Do you become easily angered, impatient, insecure, or cynical for reasons you don't understand? Do other people tell you that you tend to overreact? Do you often find yourself wondering why you got so upset? So angry? So offended? It may be that you have an attitude that you need to examine and root out.

Bad Attitudes: The Early Warning Signs

In my early days at IBM, I was working in an IBM retail products store. I was *frustrated.* I was *burned out.* I was *stressed.* My sales numbers weren't what they were expected to be. The conditions were ripe for the growth and nourishment of a bad attitude.

My boss was all over me to get my sales numbers up. I'd been hearing that since I transferred into the retail division.

If I wanted to be promoted to another division, I had to reach a certain level of sales first. So I did it. I focused and dedicated myself, and I hit the target. But nothing happened. No promotion. No pat on the back. Nothing. That discouraged me. Without even realizing it, I developed a bad attitude about the job. I'd just gotten through yet another discussion with yet another new boss who didn't like my attitude. It was not one of those shining, golden times in my life.

Turning Points to Learning Points

My cousin Kenny knew I was discouraged. He recommended that I take a class he had already been through. It was a two-and-a-half-day course called "The Pursuit of Excellence." It was one of those classes you don't know you need until you take it, but unless you take it, you'll never know you need it. Get it? I took it and I benefited. It was a wake-up call.

One of the major themes of the course was that you have to take responsibility for your attitude and for your success. It got me out of the blame game and taught me to toss the emotional baggage and attitudes that were holding me back. As part of the course, we were required to review all of the major experiences of our lives—our turning points—and recognize how the choices we made at each point shaped our lives afterward. The idea was to convert those *turning points* into *learning points*. Instead of beating yourself up over mistakes you've made or losses you've suffered, you resolve to learn from them and move on. Sure, it's easier said than done in many instances, but it's a much more constructive way to deal with life's ups and downs.

When I went back through my experiences, I realized that I had chosen the wrong attitude several times and as a result made other bad choices. I didn't let go of things, so they became baggage. In the course, they taught me to recognize my mistakes and to be accountable.

We are not permanently burdened with the baggage of our pasts. We can leave that luggage behind. It's OK to clean out the suitcases and take the good stuff that wears well—the happy memories, the hard-earned experience, the lessons learned, the joy of a first love. But the rest of it—the sad times, the loneliness, the broken heart, rejection, fear—you don't need that emotional baggage. It can only mess up your attitude and your life. Leave it on the doorstep of the past, and step into the future. History does not have to repeat itself, not if you adjust your attitude by turning away from the doors that are closed and walking through the doors that are opened to opportunity.

Three Types of Bad Attitude Baggage

To begin this mental exercise, please picture in your mind three big pieces of carry-on luggage. This is easy for me to do since I spend two-thirds of my life traveling. I don't count sheep at night. I count garment bags.

If-Only Baggage

The first piece of bad attitude baggage many people carry around is marked *If only*. This is baggage that has to do with the past. It is often full of unfinished business, plans that went awry, or hurt feelings that have not healed. It's heavy stuff. Most of the time it will not fit in the overhead compartment. In some cases the pilot will order it taken off the plane because with it he'd never be able to get liftoff.

These are some of the things you'll typically find in the *If-only* baggage.

If only:

- I'd thought before I said that.
- I hadn't had that last drink.
- I'd stayed in school.
- I'd listened to my parents.
- I'd taken precautionary measures.
- I'd spent more time with my children.
- I'd let somebody else drive.
- I hadn't given in to my desires.
- I'd kept my mouth shut.
- I hadn't tried to be the center of attention.
- I'd put more effort into the relationship
- I hadn't taken [a loved one] for granted.

The *If-only* baggage gets heavier over time because it keeps growing and growing if you don't let it go. Unless you learn to release the past, you'll eventually become so bogged down by it that you'll never move ahead.

What-Now Baggage

This emotional baggage is packed under pressure of the present. It is heavy with stress and weighty expectations. It sometimes comes packed with good news as well as bad news, but the person carrying it chooses a negative response rather than a positive one. As a result, otherwise able-bodied men and women become paralyzed.

Typical negative inner dialogue contained in *What-now* baggage goes like this:

- My spouse is unhappy. *What now?*
- I'm going to graduate with high debt. *What now?*
- We've just had twins. *What now?*
- I've been downsized. *What now?*
- I have two projects due on the same day. *What now?*

The key to dealing with this negative emotional baggage, and almost any other type of recurring stress, is to focus on opportunities and solutions rather than on potentially negative consequences or problems. You can't move quickly if you are falling under the burden of your stress and concern, so you have to lighten the load.

What-If Baggage

The third type of negative emotional baggage people commonly carry around is labeled *What-if*. It is usually packed with worries about the future, which result when people think about the potential problems ahead rather than the potential opportunities.

What if:

- I lose my job?
- I have a health problem?
- The money runs out?
- I end up alone?
- My spouse leaves me?
- The stock market crashes?
- Global warming kills us all?

There is nothing wrong in planning ahead. In fact, it would be wise to consider each of these *What-if* questions and come up with reasonable responses to each scenario. But there is a difference between focusing on the solutions to these problems and merely focusing on the problems. When we become fixated on problems, we become paralyzed. When we look ahead for solutions, we are taking responsibility and some measure of control over our lives. The danger with *What-if* baggage is that you never put it down, even when you've considered what your response might be.

The Root Causes of A Bad Attitude

Habitual bad attitudes are often the product of past experiences and events. Here are some of the most common underlying causes.

LOW SELF-ESTEEM
Do you have a habit of putting other people down? Do you tend to blame other people or circumstances for your mistakes? Do you avoid mentoring or helping other people move up in life? If so, then you've probably developed a negative attitude based on low-self esteem.

STRESS
Do you feel burned out? Do you become easily frustrated or irritated? Do you have difficulty sleeping or focusing on a single task for an extended period of time? Have you considered quitting your job, ending a relationship, or even suicide "just to get it over with"? Do you have frequent headaches, stomach problems, or back pain? These can all be signs of stress, which can trigger a poor attitude and lead to serious medical, mental, and physical problems.

I live in Atlanta, which means I have to drive in Atlanta. Look in any encyclopedia under "Atlanta traffic" and you will find a note that says, "See *Stress.*" I witness stress-induced attitudes all over the road in Atlanta. I see people getting into their cars with facial expressions very similar to those on the soldiers in the landing boats in the opening sequence of *Saving Private Ryan*. They are preparing for all-out war.

I see stressed-out attitudes every day in Atlanta, and I try to keep at least three car lengths between them and me. I used to get stressed when traffic snarled, but now I listen to motivational tapes, gospel music, and recorded Bible teachings.

FEAR

The psychologists say this word really stands for False Evidence Appearing Real. Feelings of fear are nature's alarm system for danger. The problem comes when we try to make this emotion into something real. A fear-induced attitude can render the most efficient and effective person totally useless. Fear locks you up like an engine without oil. It immobilizes you.

RESENTMENT AND ANGER

If you have a conflict with someone you work or live with, it can cause an attitude of resentment and anger that will turn your life upside down. Do you feel the urge to attack or sabotage another person or his or her property? Do you become angry just thinking about that person? Do you lose sleep because of it? Anger and resentment trigger an attitude that in the end is more harmful to you than to anyone else.

INABILITY TO HANDLE CHANGE

In a workplace transformed by rapid changes in technology, shifting demand, realignments, restructuring, corporate takeovers, and mergers, it is little wonder so many people feel threatened when a change is announced. Do you feel that failure is inevitable when faced with change? Do you get a sense of panic, loss, or betrayal? These are all the things that can affect your attitude if you are not prepared to deal with change.

We all experience those emotions at one time or another. Sometimes we get a bad attitude as a result of them. It's the inability to shake these emotions—often because they are connected to deeply rooted experiences or events—that automatically leads to a bad attitude.

The Basics of Attitude Awareness

One of the most important steps you can take toward achieving your greatest potential in life is to learn to *monitor* your attitude and its impact on your work performance, on your relationships, and on everyone around you. I generally start my seminars and workshops by asking my audiences a fundamental question: *What attitude did you bring into this meeting?* Often this brings puzzled looks. Many people close their eyes and lift their heads. That happens so often I've wondered if some folks have their Attitude of the Day written on the inside of their eyelids.

In truth, people generally don't have a high level of attitude awareness. They'll know if they are hungry. They'll know if their feet hurt. They'll know if they are attracted to the person sitting three rows up. But they usually don't have a good handle on their attitude. That is a mistake because, as it says on the cover of this book, *Attitude Is Everything*. It governs the way you perceive the world and the way the world perceives you.

The Baggage You Carry
Shapes Your Attitude

Often the most debilitating attitude we carry with us is the result of old baggage from our formative years. Since we've carried around these burdens of insecurity or low self-esteem, stress, resentment and anger, fear, and suspicion of change for so long, and since the forces behind them are buried so deep in our subconscious "basement," they are the most difficult to understand or root out.

Bad attitudes accompany those burdensome emotions because we tend to think that what has happened to us in the past will continue to happen to us for the rest of our lives. Too many people see their future in their past. It's like driving forward while looking in the rearview mirror. You may move ahead a little, but sooner or later you're going to crash.

It takes serious work to examine the roots of a harmful attitude, but the rewards of ridding ourselves of this heavy baggage can last a lifetime. I once knew a talented, attractive, and smart young lady who was constantly sabotaging her own career and relationships. She'd draw men to her and then drive them off. She'd do outstanding work but alienate her bosses and her co-workers. It was as if she couldn't help herself. She'd say mean things and pull stunts that would leave people shaking their heads at her tactics; then later she'd grow remorseful and ask for their forgiveness. She was high-maintenance as a friend and as an employee.

This talented but troubled woman was in her early thirties, before she finally identified the emotional baggage she'd been carrying around for most of her adult life. She was living with a lot of negative memories and holding on to hurtful feelings. She hadn't resolved the feelings she had toward her father and was fearful that her intimate relationships would always end in failure. Plus, she felt the pressure to be successful but feared being promoted to vice president of the firm where she worked. She was burdened with all three types of emotional baggage.

She achieved her self-discovery when she attended her first meeting of a chapter of Adult Children of Alcoholics. There she learned that the negative attitude ingrained in her mind matched very closely the typical characteristics of people who had grown up, as she had, with an alcoholic parent. Those characteristics include a victim mentality, a tendency to seek approval constantly, a powerful drive to succeed but fear of success, and difficulty in forming relationships because of low self-esteem and fear of rejection.

Only after she began attending meetings of this therapeutic service organization did my friend begin to find peace. She was able to recognize and address the attitudes that had been holding her back. She tossed out the baggage that had weighed down her life. She adopted an attitude that finally allowed her talents to manifest and her to find happiness.

Look Beneath the Surface

The rocks that lie beneath the water's surface determine whether a river runs clear and smooth or white-water rough. What lies inside of you determines the attitude you present to the world. By examining how your past experiences have shaped your attitude, you too can learn to navigate life more efficiently. When was the last time you checked the oil in your car or the air pressure in its tires? When's the last time you conducted an attitude assessment?

ATTITUDE ASSESSMENT

On a sheet of paper, make a list of the negative attitudes that may have held you back in the past. Beside each one, write down what you think the source of that attitude might be. What is the baggage and what does it contain? What past experiences? What hurt? What shame? What anger? What jealousy?

This can be a painful emotional exercise, so I advise you to go off by yourself somewhere or to ask someone who knows you well to help. A brother or sister, spouse, or parent might have clues that you can't see. This is a cleansing experience. Sometimes you have to scrape hard, so don't be afraid. And don't run from what you find. It's part of who you are. There's nothing to be ashamed of. What's past is past. Root it out, recognize it, respect it. It's a part of your life with which you need to deal.

Here are a couple of questions to ask yourself when examining your attitude, what influences it, and what impact it had or is having on your life now.

1. How do you respond to stressful situations?
This is where a bad attitude can quickly rise to the surface. When you are pressured to get something done, to perform at a higher level, or to meet high expectations, do you:

    a. Get angry
    b. Become depressed
    c. Throw up your arms in despair
    d. Get energized

Examine which of these responses is most similar to yours when you become stressed out. Then look at why you respond in that manner. What attitude drives you to respond in that way?

A friend of mine used to become highly stressed whenever he had to repair anything around the house. He had limited skills as a mechanic, plumber, or craftsman of any kind, but he realized that his stress was still unusual. One day, while stressing out as he put together a desk for his children, he flashed back to his own youth and heard his father and his brother mocking him for his lack of skills. He realized then how those deep-rooted memories had given him an insecure attitude about doing that kind of work. Because of his insecurities, he often placed too much importance on the task, tried to do it too quickly, and was highly critical of his own work even though he was no worse than the majority of amateurs.

By the way, Michael Jordan's mechanically inclined father used to tell him to "go in the kitchen with the women" when he was a boy because he was no good with a wrench or screwdriver. But he sure had some other skills that served him very well.

Look at those chores or tasks that stress you out and think about what emotions or experiences might be contributing to that stress. It's important, because stress is a killer, literally. Research reported in the *Archives of Internal Medicine* revealed that stress potentially has extremely undesirable consequences. It has been found to speed the spread of cancer, increase vulnerability to viral infections, enhance blockages in veins, accelerate the onset of diabetes, and trigger asthma attacks. Stress has also been linked to ulcers, loss of memory, and general wear and tear on the nervous system.

2. *Do you tend to look at the world in a pessimistic way?*
Pessimism is the outward expression of bad attitude. If you seem always to find the downside of an otherwise great situ-

ation, if you look for the dark lining in the silver clouds, if you see the glass as half empty rather than half full, you too may be suffering from bad-attitude-induced pessimism. Pessimists aren't much fun to be around. Or to be. They are dream-killers. Their dreams and the dreams of people around them get shot down.

A friend once complained to me that his wife was such a dream-killer. He confided that he was considering going to a marriage counselor because his wife's pessimistic attitude was taking all of the joy out of their marriage: "I'll be telling her about this great house I saw, and she'll say, 'Oh, we'll never be able to afford a place like that.' I mentioned the other day that I'd love to visit Switzerland one day, and she said, 'When would you ever have the time or money to do that?' Even when good things happen, she refuses to lighten up. I inherited $20,000 from an aunt, and her response was 'There won't be much left after we pay the bills.' When I told her that I was due for a big promotion and pay raise, she said, 'I'm not going to count my chickens before they hatch.'"

I had to concede that my friend's wife certainly did have a pessimistic view of the world. I asked him to consider what experiences or emotions might be behind her pessimistic attitude. He said he didn't know. He confronted his wife one night. He told her that she was always shooting down his dreams. They had a comfortable life, he said. What right did she have to be so pessimistic? She began weeping. She told him that her father had been a dreamer whose dreams never came true. He would often come to her and her mother and get them excited over a new invention or a new business or a new opportunity that he'd been working on, and it would always fall through. The family's finances were always close to collapse because her father's big plans never became realities.

As a result, the daughter grew up with no trust in dreams and little patience with dreamers.

My friend talked with her about those experiences and emotions from her past. He reminded his wife that he was not the same man as her father. He noted that he had been successful in achieving many of his dreams and that they'd built a comfortable life as a result of his ability to transform them into reality. She had to agree, the evidence was all around her. She began to move away from a pessimistic attitude into a more positive one. Their marriage became more enjoyable for both of them once she discarded the baggage of her past.

Toss the Baggage and Lighten the Load

It's amazing what can happen when you toss attitudinal baggage. Another friend of mine turns the sound off during certain NBA games because he can't stand the commentary of NBC sports commentator Bill Walton. It isn't that Walton doesn't know the game. The big redhead won two NCAA championships and two NBA championships in spite of being plagued by injuries that forced an early retirement. No, my friend doesn't like Walton "because he talks too darn much."

Since I'm no stranger to being wordy myself, I admire Walton. He's an Indy 500 motormouth. He squeezes more words into a twenty-second time-out than most people get into a twenty-minute conversation. He seems to take joy in every gusher of words. There just don't seem to be enough minutes in a day for him to orate, articulate, or pontificate. The other NBA commentators often joke that they can't get a word in.

I'm on Bill Walton's team. I love to hear him run off at the mouth because I know he is basking in the freedom of tossed baggage. You see, Walton was once painfully shy. He refused to speak in public. He'd run and hide from reporters even after he had played a great game because, like me, he stuttered terribly. A friend finally helped him find a speech therapist who changed Bill's life. It is such a pleasure for him finally to be able to express himself that he has a hard time keeping quiet so that other people can talk.

It's hard to get upset at Walton for jabbering when you understand the pain he endured as a high-profile athlete who was afraid to speak in public. I certainly understand.

The good news is that regardless of where you are in life, regardless of your occupation or your station, you still have the power to choose your responses and your attitude. God made you in his image, and the Lord doesn't make junk. You are a unique human being. The world has never before seen and will never see the likes of you again. You were born to bless others.

Attitude Tune-Up

- Self-awareness is the first step to becoming aware of your emotions and attitudes.
- Focus on transforming your turning points into learning points.
- What attitudinal baggage are you carrying: *If-only* baggage? *What-now* baggage? *What-if* baggage?
- The root causes of a bad attitude are low self-esteem, stress, fear, resentment, anger, and the inability to handle change.

Only the limits of our mind-set can determine the boundaries of our future.

CHAPTER FOUR

Change Your Bad Attitude for Good

STEP 4

Reframe your bad attitude.

This step will show you that a change in perspective will change your attitude, which will help you turn your attitude into action.

The car was headed for my rear bumper at about seventy miles per hour. I had nowhere to go. I was stuck in Atlanta traffic when I looked in the rearview mirror and saw it speeding up on me. Not knowing what else to do, I started honking the horn, which only bothered the poor guy in front of me. Then I heard the screeching of tires as the woman in the speeding car behind me suddenly realized that, yes, there were approximately two million other people on the road and no one was moving . . . except her.

Fortunately, her car's brakes worked. She did hit my car, but it was just a slight nudge of the rear bumper. It still scared the heck out of me, so I felt entirely justified in exercising my inalienable rights as an American commuter. I lost it. There I was, Mr. Cool, Mr. Motivation, Mr. Upbeat, yelling at this strange woman while still buckled into my seatbelt and stuck in an I–285 traffic jam.

Then I looked in my rearview mirror and saw her leaning over her steering wheel and blowing me a big kiss.

A kiss!

Talk about adjusting a guy's attitude. My inner dialogue changed course: *You are positive. You are single.*

So I blew her one back.

It's amazing how easy it is to tune up a bad attitude by making a slight adjustment in perspective. It's not always as easy as blowing a kiss, but it can be done without painful invasive surgery. When she blew the kiss at me, she wasn't being seductive. She was apologizing.

When she made the gesture, she changed my point of view. I had been thinking, *I know she's going to hit me. I hope she has insurance.* She changed my perspective when she blew me a kiss, signaling *I made a mistake, but I'm aware of it. Sorry! I'm glad you're OK! Don't be mad!*

Attitude Control 101

You can't always expect other people to adjust your attitude for you, of course. Certainly you can't expect them to do it in such a pleasant way. It's really something for which you need to take responsibility.

Most feelings wash over us and then dissolve quickly, but occasionally they strike like lightning bolts and burn deep into our hearts and souls. The death of a loved one, the breakup of a relationship, a blow to your career, an attack on your character—all of these experiences can create powerful feelings of sadness, remorse, and anger. If you don't take control of your attitude and negative emotions and find a way to ease the intensity, they can cause serious mental, physical, and spiritual deterioration.

We can take classes in school to learn how to control our finances, our careers, and even our overall successes, but where do we sign up for Attitude Control 101? A psychologist at Case Western Reserve University surveyed more than four hundred men and women, asking them what they did to control their attitudes. Nearly all of those surveyed said they were basically at the mercy of their moods. The same study found that the emotion most people had the greatest difficulty controlling was anger. Not much of a surprise there. Some people's lives are virtually controlled by inner rage. Their attitudes are expressions of that rage. They have hair-trigger tempers. They are easily offended. Staying on their good side is a high-wire act. As a result, they often have few lasting relationships.

People who are quick to anger often feel regret after they've experienced a blowup. "I'm sorry, I just lost control," they'll say. In some extreme cases of mental illness caused by a chemical imbalance, that may be true. It's also true that it is all but impossible for people caught up in a raging tantrum to return to reason immediately. They are usually beyond rational thought at that point. But in most cases, moderate anger can be controlled, and so can other emotions that carry negative consequences. Despair, grief, hatred, jealousy, resentment, fear, anxiety, and other potentially harmful feelings may sweep into our consciousness, but these troubling emotions can also be swept out. Your attitude is your responsibility.

Change Your Attitude with a Change in Perspective

A friend told me that it used to drive him crazy when he would drive home after a hard day through rush hour traffic and find the driveway to his garage impassable, blocked by his children's bicycles and toys. Nearly every day he'd have to get out and clear a path. He would lecture his kids about putting their toys away and keeping them out of the driveway, but it did no good. He even threatened to run over their toys. The kids would keep his path clear for a day or two but then fall back into their old habits. And he would get upset when he couldn't get his car into the garage after a long day of work and commuting.

Then one evening, my friend came home and once again found the driveway cluttered with Hot Wheels, sidewalk chalk, Star Wars figures, Barbie dolls, bicycles, and tricycles. He left his car at the end of the driveway, got out, and angrily began clearing a path, getting madder and madder with each toy he picked up.

At first, he didn't see his retired neighbor walk over and begin cleaning up toys alongside him. The neighbor's youngest daughter had married a few weeks earlier and moved to another state. They hadn't talked since the wedding. When my friend realized that his neighbor had joined him in the cleanup, he looked at him and muttered, "I'm sick of cleaning up behind these kids."

"Hope you don't mind if I help," the neighbor responded. "I really miss doing this now that Jamie's grown up and gone. You should enjoy it while it lasts. Your kids will be gone before you know it too. It goes so fast."

Without being aware of it—or maybe he was aware of it—the neighbor had delivered a powerful lesson. After that, my friend never again got angry when there were toys in the driveway. In fact, he said that from that point on, whenever he came home he felt gratitude when he saw bicycles and Barbie dolls spread out all over his driveway. "The kids are still kids. I've got more time with them," he now thinks.

The driveway still looks like Toys "R" Us after an earthquake. His children are not putting their toys away. Nothing has changed but his perspective. Yet his attitude has changed dramatically. My friend simply learned to reframe the situation. He substituted gratitude for anger and changed his attitude for good.

You Determine the Value of Your Experiences

Have you ever thought about the true value of a one hundred dollar bill? What would it be worth if you were alone on a desert island? Only the little shade it might provide, right? Without someone willing to trade you goods or a service for that one hundred dollar bill, it is worthless. Its worth is only what someone else is willing to give you in exchange for it. Otherwise, it's just a piece of paper. The bill's value depends on your point of view.

It's the same with pretty much everything in the world and everything that happens to you. If you lose your job, the experience has only the value you give it. You can take an attitude of defeat and anger, or you can take the attitude that you are now free to explore other options or to do what you have always wanted to do. It is a matter of perception. It's up to you to assign a value or meaning to it based on the point of view you decide to take.

If the idea of tuning up your attitude by changing your perspective sounds a little too easy to you—maybe a little Pollyannaish—think for a moment about some of the worst things that happened to you in childhood, those things that seemed like terrible tragedies at the time. Your dog died. You fell off your bicycle and broke your front teeth. You kicked a ball through a church's stained glass window. You got called to the principal's office.

Now reflect on those things. Didn't you learn something about life? Didn't new opportunities arise even if something was lost? Didn't some benefits come of those experiences too?

There are benefits to be found in almost anything that happens to you. Sometimes they are not always obvious right away, but if you take a long-term perspective and understand that what is happening right now is only a temporary thing, you will be less likely to become embittered or to form a negative attitude because of things that happen to you.

Some things that happen to you may seem impossible to deal with or to reframe at first. The death of a loved one, for example, triggers grief, a very powerful emotion. Just when you think you've learned to "handle it," grief can resurface unexpectedly. At first, it can seem unbearable, but it's not permanent. Believe it or not, grief follows a well-charted course. There are many great books on the process of grief, and a grief counselor can help you deal with it effectively. So can loved ones. I'm not suggesting that it will be easy. It never is. There are ways to reframe the grieving experience, though. I've found that it helps me to take the perspective that the loved one I've lost would want me to go on with life and to enjoy its blessings for as long as I am given.

What you allow yourself to think about your grief or depression can either make it better or worse. Again, you and I have very little control over what happens to us in this chaotic world, but we do have the power to control our responses to what happens and the attitudes we present to the world. We are not helpless.

I came home from playing basketball at the gym one day when I was thirteen years old and found my father packing his bags. He called me into the bedroom and said, "I've got to leave. Your mom and I have not gotten along in years. I'm going to live somewhere else. We'll be getting a divorce."

I didn't know what to say. I used to shut my door and put pillows over my head so I couldn't hear them arguing. My sister would try to stop them. She's now a police captain, by the way, still serving as a "peace officer." I asked my dad if he would give me a ride back to the gym. Looking back, I think I just wanted to find a way to spend a little more time with him. I felt guilty that he was leaving, as if I hadn't done my job. I was full of guilt and regret. *It was my fault they didn't get along.*

We didn't say much on the way to the gym. I felt I understood. I thought I could handle it. I remember getting out of the car saying, "I'll see you later, Dad." It was all I could think to say.

Divorce was not such a common thing back then. I felt both guilt and shame. When my friends asked where my dad was, I'd tell them he was sick or on vacation. I lost interest in basketball, my friends, and school. I was quiet, but my inner conversation wasn't. *I'll never get over this. My entire life is ruined! Why didn't I do something to keep them together?*

My grandmother, bless her, saw me moping around and picked up on it. "You're holding onto something," she said. "It's not your fault that they split up."

I asked her if she could get my father back with my mom. My grandmother knew it was best for this marriage to end. She told me that my parents would never get back together, but they were still my mother and father. I told her I was worried that my father would move away and forget me. "He has moved out," she said, "but he is never going to move away or forget you."

My grandmother, in her wisdom, took the burden of my parents' divorce off my shoulders. She saw that I had personalized the breakup of my parent's marriage, which is common for children going through a divorce. She also noted that I had interpreted my father's move from the house as if he were moving entirely out of my life, so she assured me that was not the case. She helped me see that my life was not going to change dramatically, that there was still a strong foundation of family to support me.

She told me that I could still go to my father because he would probably need me more than ever. She said my mother too would be looking to me for support and love. My grandmother did me a great favor that day. She not only helped me deal with my parents' divorce, she also gave me a primary lesson in managing my emotions and adjusting my attitude.

The Three-P's That Cause Bad Attitudes

There are three points to remember when faced with a major challenge. If you keep them in mind, you will get back on your feet much quicker, and you will be far less likely to develop a negative attitude as a result of bad experiences. Remember that the challenge is not:

1: *Permanent*. It's not going to last forever.

Why is it that when something wonderful happens to us we immediately fear that the joy won't last, but when something tragic occurs we immediately assume that we will never get over it? Why aren't we better at savoring the good times and letting go of the bad? It does take time to recover from bad things that happen to us. The process can often be difficult. But there is a process. It's part of our emotional makeup. The subconscious mind runs you through it on autopilot as long as you don't insist on wallowing in self-pity and grief. What good does that do anyone? Give yourself over to the recovery process, knowing that over time you will transform this turning point into a learning point.

2: *Pervasive.* It's not going to destroy your entire life.

When I didn't get drafted to play professional basketball, I initially thought that my dreams and goals of accomplishing success in my life were over. I felt the respect I had earned as an athlete couldn't be replaced. Looking back, not playing professional basketball was a blessing in disguise. That experience of dramatic change taught me how to embrace change in all areas of my life.

3: *Personal.* You are not the only one this happens to.

I can see personalizing license plates. I can see personalizing address tags. But why do we personalize the bad things that happen to us? Life is random. Everything is not personal. Yet we don't seem to get it. *Why does this always happen to me? Why can't I ever catch a break? What did I do to deserve this?* Get over it. It's not about you. It's about life. Some days you're going to be a bug on the windshield of life. Some days you'll find the nectar in its flowers. Did you ever see a golf course without hazards? You won't see a life without them either. You aren't alone in your misery *or* your joy. Be glad that you are a part of it all. Take comfort that your experiences are universal. Rise to the challenges and develop the skills necessary to survive and thrive.

When you're working all three P's, psychologists say you've adopted an attitude of "learned helplessness." Bad things happen to good people. Some get hit with tragedy after tragedy. Others walk through life virtually unscathed. Understand that life is going to hand you challenges. It may even seem to knock you down to the ground sometimes. You don't have much choice in that. But you do have control over how you respond. You must have faith that you will overcome.

The Power of Words

The things we say and the things we hear from others are another great cause of a bad attitude. Whether said in love or in anger, words leave a lasting impression. Therefore you should be very mindful of the things you say, particularly in anger. Once released to the universe, words cannot be taken back.

Gratitude and Forgiveness: The Antidotes to Negative Attitude

I read a magazine story about a married couple who were devastated initially when they learned that their youngest child had Down's syndrome. They grieved because they felt the child would never have a normal or happy life, which to them meant being accepted, being self-sufficient, and having a fulfilling life. "Why did this happen to us?" they asked.

As the parents learned more about Down's syndrome and as the child grew older, their perspective changed. They began to see that this child had a joyful, loving spirit. He had his own unique outlook on what constituted a fulfilling life. When he won a race at the Special Olympics, he was thrilled beyond words. In time the parents came to feel that they had been blessed to have such a child. "Our lives are richer because of this young man and what he has taught us about unconditional love," they concluded.

Instead of being saddened about what had happened to them, this couple learned to feel gratitude. Their adjustment did not occur overnight. True wisdom rarely comes in lightning bolts. They had to deal with a wide range of emotions including disappointment, grief, and fear. Those feelings came to them, but they did not allow them to live within them. As a result, their attitudes eventually became far more positive and constructive.

When your car runs low on fuel, you go to the service station and fill the tank so you can keep going, right? When your cell phone battery loses power, you plug it back into the power source, don't you? Why is it, then, that when your emotions and attitude take a downward plunge, you don't look to your own source of rejuvenation?

We all have a reserve of positive memories and emotions that we can tap into during challenging times. The source that I plug into is God. For some reason, we seem to plug into negative sources more often. In sad times, we tend to plug into emotions like regret, helplessness, and sorrow rather than recharging our attitudes with more empowering feelings.

Two of the best antidotes to a negative attitude are gratitude and forgiveness. When the couple with the Down's syndrome child learned to feel gratitude rather than disappointment and fear, they moved from an attitude of hurting to one of healing. The same thing occurred with the father who had been angry because he couldn't get past the toys to his garage. Their lives became happier and richer with that simple exchange of emotions.

It is deceptively simple, isn't it? All it takes is exchanging one mind-set for another. When you stop blaming and criticizing or feeling hurt and angry, you are then free to forgive and love, to be grateful and accepting. There's so much to be grateful for. I try not to take anything for granted. Each day I try to count at least a hundred things I'm grateful for. I find that it improves my attitude for the entire day. Knowing you're blessed allows you to attain a level of patience, understanding, and joy. When you focus on your challenges instead, you become unsettled, impatient, and unhappy.

What others do to you doesn't cause your bad attitude. Your own thoughts and the emotions you allow to live within you cause it. If you allow yourself to be grateful and forgiving, you'll be able to let go of pride, ego (which stands for Edging God Out), anger, vindictiveness, criticism, judgment, and hurt.

We demand an awful lot from others, more than we usually demand of ourselves. If we accept that we are human and make mistakes and misjudgments, we should be willing to forgive others.

A few years ago I rushed to judgment on the two people who were working in my office, managing my bookings, travel arrangements, and financial affairs. The business was growing very quickly, and they had become overwhelmed. One of them had health problems that added to the burden. Since I was traveling constantly, I did not see that they were overloaded, but I could detect that there were problems. I brought in some consultants to make recommendations. My staff wouldn't follow their directives. I felt they had the wrong attitudes. Realistically, they weren't equipped to handle the business because of its explosive growth. When things didn't work out, I decided to let an outside firm manage my business. They doubled the people in the office, but we experienced many of the same problems.

At that point I realized I'd been harsh in my judgment of my original staff, who had been very loyal to me. I went to the two individuals and asked for their forgiveness.

Forgiving each other allowed us to work together again. We became closer and developed mutual respect. We learned to appreciate our respective strengths and weaknesses. We reached a real sense of inner peace because there was no bitterness or hurt. We realized that we shared the same goals, and we created an environment in which we worked together to find ways to achieve those goals.

It's important to forgive people. Forgiveness does not require you to maintain relationships with harmful and hurtful individuals. If you've been abused physically or emotionally, forgive them in your heart. Forgiveness releases you from the pain and the anger. It allows you to release negative feelings and replace them with a spirit of peace. You can have a loving attitude from a distance.

Self-forgiveness is important too. Some people find it difficult to forgive themselves because they're perfectionists. They've set an unrealistic standard. We all need to realize we're not perfect. In college when I became very ill, I had to adopt an attitude of self-forgiveness. I was mad at myself for being sick and not being able to do anything about it.

Last year, I met a young woman who shared her story of self-forgiveness. For five years, Stacey had been addicted to drugs. She'd quit for a while and then return to her destructive behavior. Her breakthrough came when a counselor made her look him in the eye and tell him how she felt about herself and her life. It was the beginning of self-acceptance. She said that for the first time in her life she had to take a close look at who she was and to confront her guilt and her fear. Most of her life, she'd been afraid that she wouldn't like herself. Then one day she wrote a letter to herself apologizing for her behavior, for keeping people at a distance, and for not loving herself. Once she forgave herself, she had the courage and the strength to stop using drugs. She says that each day she asks God to help her continue to do her best.

Here are other important points to consider when tapping into the power of forgiveness.

- *There is no statute of limitations on forgiveness.*
  If there is a situation requiring forgiveness that occurred during your childhood, or years ago, it is still necessary to work through those negative feelings. Negativity allowed to fester will affect all aspects of your life. It is a cancer that will grow and spread unless you learn to forgive and release the bitterness and anger.
- *Expect suspicion when you go to forgive.*
  You can't expect the other person to understand immediately that you have made the leap from bitterness to forgiveness. Approach the person in a nonthreatening way. Allow the person room to maneuver and time to think.
- *If you have missed your opportunity and the other person is gone, it's still necessary to forgive.*
  Try writing a letter to that person and one to yourself. Visualize yourself offering forgiveness to him or her. Tell them how they hurt you. Be very specific. Tell them you forgive them and that you have released your anger.
- *Don't deny, ignore, or try to overlook a hurtful memory.*
  Are there old hurts or grudges that you're still harboring from years ago? Go back and uncover those areas and address them. If you don't, you will unconsciously carry

an attitude that will reflect the hurt and anger you are holding in.

- *Understand that forgiveness may not be mutual.*
When you're asking for forgiveness, remember that you can't control the other person's response. If the person won't forgive you, forgive yourself and move on.

Give Yourself Permission to Love and Forgive

My relationship with my father always seemed a little distant. I hungered for his approval, and he didn't easily give it. The son of a blue-collar worker, he improved his life through hard work and intellectual challenges and became a college professor. He believed his role was to push me, not praise me. If I came home with C's and B's on my report card, he would say, "You can do better." If I told him I'd scored twenty points in a game, he'd say the competition must not have been real strong. I didn't understand it then, but my dad was pushing me to achieve at a higher level and trying to keep me humble.

My buddy Dan Clark gave a speech on the power of effective communications. Dan said, "The next time we give this seminar, let's take a survey and ask how many men have heard their fathers say, 'I love you.'" That night I realized that I had never heard my father tell me he loved me. Later that night I called my grandma and talked to her about it. She said something to me I'll never forget. "I know your daddy loves you, but looking back, I don't think his father ever told him."

Sometimes in life, when you want something you have to be willing to take the initiative. I decided that on my dad's birthday I'd call and tell him "I love you." If you want more friends, you've got to be a friend. If you want love, you've got to give love. As a result of that one birthday call, my father and I regularly tell each other "I love you."

Three of the strongest motivating words in the world happen to be the three least used: *I love you.* Do you know someone who is overdue to hear those words?

Letting go of blame, hurt, and anger and replacing those negative emotions with an attitude of forgiveness and gratitude is a powerfully healing experience. It also returns responsibility for your life back to you. It's no longer anyone else's fault that you haven't accomplished your dreams or achieved your goals. Once the blaming stops, you accept responsibility. I think that not wanting to accept responsibility is why so many people hide behind negative attitudes.

It may be true that someone else is responsible for something that happened to you, but once you've identified that person, what purpose does it serve to continue blaming him or her? Let go of the blame, forgive, and take back the responsibility for your life. Tell yourself that you have the power to heal through forgiveness and gratitude. Be accountable. Begin today to forgive those people in your life who have caused you anguish or pain.

My friend Janelle shared her story of forgiveness with me. She and her father had a tense relationship. He expected her to fit his image of the "proper" female. He felt she should have gotten married and stayed home to raise children, but she didn't. She's single, independent, and a well-educated professional. As a result, she has rarely received his approval. He became upset with her and refused to speak to her about the situation.

Janelle has a forgiving heart. Even though she had been treated poorly by her father, she took the initiative and wrote him a letter to try and open communication with him. He refused to read it. She wrote another letter. He didn't read that one either.

When his birthday came, she sent him a large bouquet of flowers with a card saying, "Daddy, I love you." That kind gesture opened the lines of communication. They had a loving, painfully honest, emotional talk.

She forgave him.

Many times we take on an attitude of helplessness in these situations. *What can I do, he won't respond? I've done all I can. It's up to him now to reach out.* Since Janelle was willing to humble herself and to choose love over frustration and anger, there was a breakthrough.

> *Love is patient and kind;*
> *it is not jealous or conceited or proud;*
> *love is not ill-mannered or selfish or irritable;*
> *love does not keep a record of wrongs;*
> *love is not happy with evil;*
> *but is happy with the truth.*
> *Love never gives up; . . .*
> *Love is eternal.*
>
> —I CORINTHIANS 13:4–8

Attitude Tune-Up

- Attitude Control 101: Your attitude is your responsibility. Start managing your emotions.
- You can change your attitude with a change in perspective.
- You determine the value of your life's experiences.

- The three P's that cause bad attitudes: believing that bad luck is *permanent, pervasive,* and *personal.*
- Gratitude and forgiveness—the important elements for maintaining a positive attitude.

Remember that your real wealth is measured not by what you have, not by where you are, but by the spirit that lives within you.

CHAPTER FIVE

Turn Attitude Into Action!

STEP 5
Find your purpose and passion.

This step will help you understand the power of living your life with a clear purpose and passion. It helps you create the vision, goals, and plans you need to turn attitude into action.

In my first seven years at IBM, I was eager to please but I didn't have any direction for my career within the company. I was just hoping to find a comfortable and secure place, probably as a salesman, someday. At first, I was excited just to be at Big Blue. Basketball hadn't worked out. I obviously wasn't cut out to be an apprentice painter in Alaska. Given my lack of other options, I felt fortunate to be granted a job by one of America's most admired and powerful companies.

It didn't take long for my attitude to change. It deteriorated into feelings of frustration and resentment. *Why didn't I get a better territory? Their sales numbers weren't any better than mine. I'll never get promoted.*

Some people join a company and begin swiftly climbing up the corporate ladder. My ladder ran out of rungs, and I joined the IBMalcontent club. I had a long list of excuses for my lack of success. IBM had risen to the top of the Fortune 500 because of its world-famous sales force. For thirty years, electric typewriters had been Big Blue's primary product, but that was twenty years before I came on the scene. High-tech mainframe computers were the company's bread and butter when I was hired. Yet I was posted to a low-tech office equipment division where I rarely made a sale, so I couldn't make my quota, which made me a noncandidate for promotion, according to IBM's policies.

All Dressed Up with No Passion or Purpose to Go

I had done my best to fit into the company culture. I wore the right suits, shirts, and ties. I had the sales patter down pat. But my inner dialogue was self-defeating. *Maybe I'm in the wrong business. Maybe I'm just not cut out for sales.* In my mind, the source of my problems was always external. The negative inner dialogue was the result of a poor attitude, which itself was a symptom of a deeper problem.

It wasn't IBM. It wasn't my bosses. It wasn't my job or my co-workers. It was me. As I've noted in previous chapters, often a bad attitude is due to the emotional baggage we carry with us from one stage of life to the next. Sometimes, though, our negative attitudes aren't products of our past. They can also be an expression of our fear of the future.

When we feel trapped, bogged down, stuck in the mud, and going no place fast, we develop bad attitudes. Then we fall into the blame game. We find fault with everyone and everything around us. Once again, the enemy usually lies within.

Many times we get stuck because we don't know where we want to go in the first place. Think about the happiest people you know, the people with the most positive, energized attitudes in your school, on the team, in your office, in your family, and in your community. They may be from different walks of life, in different stages of their careers, but it's highly likely that they have two things in common. Those positively charged people are working on goals (*purpose*) while doing what they love (*passion*).

When I set my sights on getting a job with Big Blue, I did it with a very limited vision. I wanted security. I wanted the prestige of working for an internationally recognized corporation. I hadn't given up after not making the NBA. I had looked for new opportunities and worked hard to pursue them. But my vision was shortsighted. I'd set a goal with no passion or purpose behind it. I wanted to have a job at IBM—period. No wonder I became frustrated once I got inside the company door.

Living for a Purpose

What happened to me at IBM is a case study of how a change in attitude can change your life.

I'd been a marketing representative in the IBM Product Center Store in Seattle for nearly three years when my regional manager told me that it was time I moved into another position. He was right. I was burned out. It was just a job to me. A safe, secure job, but hardly one I could get excited about. I was doing just well enough to hold onto the job and not badly enough to be fired, which isn't saying much, since at that point IBM still prided itself on retaining its people.

I was in a rut and had no idea of what else I was qualified to do within the company. My self-confidence was at an all-time low. Fortunately, there were a few people within the company who saw more in me than I saw in myself. Since I'd won a marketing excellence award for my sales presentation skills, my regional manager thought I might make a good training instructor for the company.

Training instructors conduct classes for new IBM employees, teaching them sales and marketing techniques as well as the basics of IBM products. I'd been through most of the training programs. I'd had some great instructors who could make the most mundane class interesting, and I'd had others whose classes were like watching paint dry. So I had a fair idea of what worked and didn't work for a trainer. A friend of mine, Ervin Smith, an instructor, thought I would be a good instructor too. He had recommended me to his boss, who talked with my regional manager and invited me to fill in for two weeks as a guest instructor in Atlanta.

My negative inner dialogue kicked in as soon as they told me about it. *Will I be able to master the technical material in such a short time? I won't be able to answer questions from all of those smart trainees.* Comfort zones can be treacherous. I wasn't even *that* comfortable as a marketing rep. I just didn't want to leave the familiar for the unfamiliar, no matter how frustrated I was. It was not where I wanted to be, but I didn't see any particularly enticing options anywhere else.

I wasn't happy where I was, but I didn't know what I wanted to do. I was angry about standing still but afraid to move. A great many people are in the same situation. They hang onto dissatisfying, dead-end jobs because they are afraid to make a move. Here's a news flash for them: If you don't make a move, sooner or later, life makes a move on you.

That's exactly what happened to me. My regional manager took me to lunch one day to break it to me gently. "You aren't going anywhere as a marketing rep," he said. "You've got to go see if you can make it as a trainer in Atlanta. That's an order."

Once the boss kicked me out of the comfort zone and made it clear that I was going to Atlanta whether I liked it or not, I woke up and changed my approach. I became Mr. Positive Attitude. "If I go down there, I won't let you down," I told him. "I will be the best. I will do the job better than anyone has ever done it."

By the time I got to the Atlanta training school, I was pumped up. I was determined that no one was going to nod off, complete a crossword puzzle, or write a doctoral thesis during my classes. I wanted their full attention, and I was going to earn it. It was show time, and I was the headliner. Strange things happen when you leave a comfort zone and turn your attitude into action.

Once I got up in front of those raw IBM recruits, I knew that I'd found my passion.

There was one problem. IBM didn't need a trainer in Atlanta at that particular moment. When I told my bosses I'd found my purpose and passion, I ran right into a wall of bureaucratic brick. "There aren't any openings in that position right now, and besides, you know that IBM promotes people based on performance. Your sales numbers aren't that great. You aren't even the top salesperson in your store!"

I'd been ready to pack my bags for Georgia. Instead, the old bad attitude baggage was handed back to me. Even worse, a new manager was sent to our store. He suggested I might be put on probation if my sales numbers didn't get better. This new manager hadn't read my personnel file so he didn't know about my stint as a trainer. He didn't know that I was dejected because I had found my purpose and passion only to run into a roadblock.

Before I could convince the boss that I wasn't a deadbeat, another bomb dropped. IBM sold its stores. It was getting out of the retail business. If I wanted to stay with the company, I had to go back for forty weeks of intense training in mainframe sales. Basically, they were asking me to start from scratch. If I didn't do well in my classes, I'd probably be tossed out the door.

I was discouraged as I began the training classes, but there was something about the training environment that stirred up the fire in me again. I was fascinated by the techniques of the instructors. Some were not all that good, but I learned a bit from each of them. Working in the retail stores was challenging, but being in the classroom lifted my spirits. It gave me a new focus and purpose—to become an IBM training instructor.

Have you heard the saying "When the student is ready, the teacher will appear"? My new boss was a young guy, Craig Kairis, who had trained under me as a new IBM hire. We'd established a rapport and remained friends. His first words to me when he came to work as my boss were "This company doesn't recognize your talent. I'm going to help you show them!"

Throughout my career at IBM, I had a support team. Craig had been part of that team since his first years with the company. From the minute Craig became my manager, we sat down and mapped out a strategic plan to realize my goal of becoming a training instructor. He was in charge of a major IBM product announcement that all of the employees in the region were to attend. Craig arranged for me to be a presenter, to showcase my speaking skills. During my brief twenty-minute presentation, I raised the level of enthusiasm in the room. If you'd been standing outside the meeting room, you would have sworn there was a spiritual revival going on. I had those salespeople on their feet, shouting *Hallelujah!*

The one person who didn't make the meeting was the branch manager who'd been blocking my attempts to become an IBM sales school instructor. When he returned from vacation, there was an e-mail message from *his* boss wanting to know who Keith Harrell was and why he wasn't conducting every product introduction meeting and teaching others how to do it.

In the weeks that followed, I got call after call from managers around the region wanting me to do program events for them. Meanwhile, back in my sales territory, my numbers were up because Craig was giving me support like I'd never had before.

I had purpose. I had passion. I was on a roll. At the end of the year, my name came up for promotion, but the branch manager again stepped in my path. He insisted that I complete one year on a large account team in mainframe computer sales because he thought that would enhance my career. But Craig had been working behind the scenes, promoting my talents to the other members of the management team. When the branch manager balked at letting me go, the other managers outvoted him. The rest of the management team stood up for me. They saw that I had a purpose and a passion, and they bought into my vision.

Lack of Vision Will Get You Lost

Have you shared your vision with those who might help you? Write down what you want to do, for whom, and for what purpose. Make a chart of how you intend to pursue your vision. The "how" will help you put your attitude into action. People who don't understand the importance of goals are always running into walls. They have a poor attitude because of their shortsightedness. They are out of synch with life. They don't know what they want, so they aren't prepared when opportunities arise.

Write this on your hands, on your bedroom ceiling, on your forehead (backward if you tend to look in the mirror): *You have to know what you want before you can go after it!* When you go shopping, do you walk around the mall, identify every item that you don't want, and then buy what's left? Or do you go there knowing what you want, find it, and buy it? Why would you lead your life any differently? Why would you go to work for a corporation, play on a sports team, be in a relationship, or live your life without some sense of purpose, direction, or goal? As that great wise man, philosopher, and catcher Yogi Berra once said, "If you don't know where you are going, you might wind up someplace else."

Going goalless is like trying to drive to an unfamiliar address in a new town without a road map or directions. You might eventually get where you're going, but chances are you'll pull over in frustration or settle for a "suitable" substitute. To avoid being bounced around, you need to set priorities. Goals are the means for doing that.

We all share certain goals. Once we have the basic goals of food, shelter, clothing, and cable television covered, we begin to set other goals that are more specific to our unique nature and our priorities. When you have well-defined goals, you are far less likely to develop a bad attitude. If you suspect that you are carrying around a negative attitude because you've arrived someplace other than where you really want to be, then it's time to sit down with paper and pen and do a little soul- and goal-searching. Here is a quick attitude assessment designed to determine if you're suffering from a lack of purpose and passion.

ATTITUDE ASSESSMENT

NEGATIVE INNER DIALOGUE
CAUSED BY BEING—

GOALLESS AT WORK

- I'm going nowhere here.
- Why are they holding me back?
- Why won't they recognize my good work?
- My quotas are impossible.
- Even if I'm a top performer, they won't reward me.
- I don't care if I get promoted or not, I'm just here for the paycheck.

GOALLESS AT SCHOOL

- I can study later.
- My grades are passing.
- Why do I have to take the course? I'll never use this information.
- There aren't enough hours in the day to read this material.

GOALLESS IN YOUR PERSONAL LIFE

- I'm too old.
- Is this it?
- I can't seem to get out of debt.
- I can't seem to get ahead.
- I'm too young.

If any of that self-talk sounds familiar, you may be lacking purpose, and most definitely passion, in one or more of these areas. You'll notice that there's a lot of blaming going on in those bits of dialogue. When you hear that in your inner dialogue, the bad attitude alarms should go off. Those are the early warning signs that you've abdicated your primary responsibility to take charge of your life.

Goals are tools for focusing your life, taking responsibility, and getting you to take action. Achieving goals is just part of what is really important—the quality of life you experience, the person you become, and the difference you make in the lives of others as you pursue and achieve your goals.

It's Not the Destination, It's the Journey

I discovered the principle behind that philosophy while playing basketball in high school. When we won the state championship, it dawned on me that getting the title and the trophy wasn't the real reward. It was the season-long experience of being with guys who played well together, improved together, and then celebrated each other's contributions to the winning effort. Realizing that did wonders for my attitude. I always felt that I was working on something. The sense of being in control gave me energy and focus.

When I went to work for IBM, I hadn't taken the time to identify my purpose or my passion. Instead of taking responsibility for my life, I was looking for shelter. I'd just lost my passion for basketball and my purpose, playing in the NBA. I was still recovering from that disappointment.

Some people are fortunate enough to identify a passion early on and then build their goals and their lives around pursuing that passion. Often they are people with the most obvious talents: writers, musicians, athletes, singers, mechanics, chefs, and others whose natural gifts are easily channeled into a life's purpose.

When I lost the opportunity to play basketball professionally, I thought I'd lost my purpose and passion. I spent several years wandering around with an attitude of disappointment at IBM before I realized that I hadn't lost them, I'd only misplaced them.

Looking back, I can see now that I came close to discovering my real passion once or twice. About a year before I was sent to be a guest trainer, I got a call at work late on a Friday afternoon from an IBM manager. She was frantic. There was a Career Day for five hundred high-achieving minority high school seniors—all of them standouts in math and science—that weekend. IBM's representative, a systems engineer, had been scheduled to speak but she'd had to cancel because of a family emergency. They needed someone to replace her. Would I go?

My initial response was *You want me? I didn't major in science or math in college.* Then it dawned on me. There were two obvious reasons I'd been called:

> *No. 1:* It's Friday. Everybody else has probably
> already gone home or made plans for the weekend.
> *No. 2:* It's a *minority* Career Day.

Based on those two criteria, I was the perfect man for the job. I also didn't have a good excuse for turning them down, and I figured it might help raise my profile at IBM and in the community. The Career Day was to be held the next day from 9 A.M. until noon on the University of Washington campus. The next morning I woke up at 7 A.M. in a panic. I called my best buddy at IBM, Ralph Bianco, and asked him what I should talk about. He told me to tell the story of how I went from hoping to play pro basketball to not getting drafted and then to preparing myself for an IBM job. "It's a good story about winning and losing and setting yourself up for opportunities. Why don't you talk about attitude? You're always talking about the difference it makes," Ralph said.

When I arrived at the Career Day, I ran into Robert Lee, my high school math teacher, who was in charge of the event. He was happy to see me. The other speakers were an imposing bunch: local celebrities, public officials, and businesspeople from a wide range of professions. Each person was allotted twenty minutes to talk and five minutes to answer questions. I was way down on the schedule, so I took a seat in the back of the auditorium. The first few people were so inspiring I began to take notes. I was getting more out of it than most of the kids. I didn't see any of them taking notes, and most of them looked bored. As I listened, I got excited because nobody was really talking about the things I wanted to cover.

The adrenaline was really starting to flow as my turn drew near. Just before I was supposed to speak, Robert Lee made an announcement: "I'm sorry, but because our speakers have been so enthusiastic, we've run out of time," he said. "We won't be able to get to the remaining speakers, but we appreciate their coming this morning."

Before I realized what I was doing, I was on my feet. "We can't stop now," I yelled from the back of the room. "You can't wrap it up, Mr. Lee. I've got some things I want to share."

My old teacher realized that I was on a mission. "It looks like perhaps we've saved our best speaker for last," he told the group.

I talked for thirty minutes nonstop. I told the students

what I had learned about self-esteem, motivation, and the power of attitude. I was in a zone.

When I finished, they gave me a standing ovation. One woman came up and said, "You remind me of some of the motivational speakers at the Amway conventions!"

Dreams with Deadlines

I was fired up about public speaking after that Career Day appearance, but I didn't go anywhere with the passion that it stirred. I didn't have the vision to see what I could do with my natural-born ability for public speaking. I simply didn't connect that passion to any purpose or goal. It took me more than a year to see how I could channel my passion for public speaking into a purpose as a trainer at IBM.

It's up to you to set goals and direct your passion at a purpose. Start making changes today that will get you to where you want to be tomorrow. Dare to dream, and then set deadlines for realizing those dreams.

Take some quiet time today and write down your dreams for your life. What do you enjoy doing? What can you do for hours and hours and enjoy so much that you lose track of time? What are you better at than anyone you know? It doesn't have to be a great and unique talent like playing the harp or building skyscrapers. The level of your talent isn't nearly as important as the intensity of your passion.

I will never be the orator that the Rev. Martin Luther King, Jr. was, but I can do my best to be what God has blessed me to be. I encourage you to do the same. Maybe you have musical talent and want to share that gift with others. There are many paths to pursue, including performing, teaching, composing, recording, publishing, selling, or booking musical talent.

When you've identified your purpose and passion, put a deadline on it. Don't make it a vague wish. You don't want to say, "I want to make a lot of money soon." That won't get you anywhere. Instead, set a goal of making an exact amount by an exact date. The more specific, the better.

Once you have defined your goal or goals, make a list of smaller goals that can be achieved in the short term. These are the mini-goals that will take you step-by-step toward your greater goals. Date the smaller goals. If your goal is to go back to school and get your MBA, set mini-goals for raising the tuition or applying for a scholarship. Other mini-goals for that major goal might be selecting a school, getting an application form, filling it out and submitting it, and selecting a course of study. Or maybe your goal is to get a promotion at work. Your mini-goals could include selecting the position you want to be promoted to, talking with your supervisors about what you need to do to get that job, and then setting those tasks as mini-goals along the way.

CREATE A WORK-LIFE GAME PLAN

1. After writing down your long-term career goal, next list a series of step-by-step specific positions you want to reach with specific salary levels for each.
2. Create mini-goals that add value to your résumé, such as a more advanced degree, special training, team projects, or management experiences that will prepare you for the next level.
3. Put deadlines on each set of goals and mini-goals, starting with one month and then going to three months, six months, one year, three years, five years, eight years, and ten years.

4. For each mini-goal, write a positive affirmation (I'll show you how in Chapter 7) stating why the goal is important to you and how it will help you move closer to your primary goal.

Here is a blueprint to assist you in designing your own Work-Life Game Plan.

David's goal is to become a regional director of sales in ten years. As a recent college graduate, he's starting at an entry-level position within the corporation.

Primary Long-Term Goal: I will be promoted to regional director of sales.

1. Sales Associate, $30,000   ONE YEAR
   One-month objective: Successfully complete training class.
   Affirmation: I am the best trainee in my class because I'm very attentive and practice my sales presentations every evening. I'm always willing to help others.
   Three-month objective: Exceed sales quota by 5 percent.
   Affirmation: I will exceed my sales quota by doing a solid direct mail campaign.
   Six-month objective: Be promoted to sales rep.
   Affirmation: I am a great sales rep because I provide excellent customer service.

2. Sales Rep, $45,000   ONE YEAR
   One-month objective: Successfully complete training class.
   Affirmation: I am excited to be a sales rep because I can operate my territory like it's my own business.
   Three-month objective: Have thorough knowledge of all products. Develop business plan.
   Affirmation: I am a knowledgeable sales rep because I stay current on the latest technology.

Six-month objective: Find a mentor or coach in the branch office to help me with my marketing skills.

Affirmation: I have a great coach and mentor who is teaching me the advanced marketing skills I need to enhance my success.

One-year objective: Exceed my quota by 10 percent in the next six months.

Affirmation: I am exceeding my quota by 10 percent by utilizing all my branch resources.

3. Marketing Rep, $50,000   TWO YEARS

One-month objective: Exceed sales quota by 15 percent.

Affirmation: I will provide superior service to all my customers by understanding their industry and business needs.

Three-month objective: Enroll in outside courses to help me understand my customers' industries.

Affirmation: I am becoming an industry expert. My customers view me as a consultant who brings value to their businesses.

Six-month objective: Develop leadership and management skills.

Affirmation: I am an effective team leader, and I manage my time and resources wisely.

One-year objective: Win the Marketing Excellence Award and greatly exceed my quota objectives by 20 percent.

Affirmation: I am one of the top marketing reps in the region and will be promoted to advisory rep.

4. Advisory Rep, $55,000–$65,000   ONE YEAR

One-month objective: Successfully complete business plan for making quota and managing new territory.

Affirmation: I've completed my plan. I am exceeding my quota and managing my territory.

Three-month objective: Enhance my technical, negotiation, and communication skills in order to position myself as a leader in the branch office.

Affirmation: I am an effective communicator, a great negotiator, and a technical resource for all the people in the branch as well as the rest of the region.

Six-month objective: Enhance my selling techniques and entrepreneurial skills and learn more about the financial aspects of the business.

Affirmation: I will improve my financial and advanced selling skills.

One-year objective: Take on a larger territory and sell more advanced products to larger customer groups in order to position myself for promotion. Make the Gold Circle, which is awarded to the top 10 percent of salespeople who have achieved their quota objectives.

Affirmation: I will effectively manage a larger territory and exceed my quota by 25 percent.

5. Regional Staff Position, $70,000–$75,000   ONE YEAR

One-month objective: Learn the fundamentals of running the business at the regional staff level.

Affirmation: I am successfully running the business at the regional staff level.

Three-month objective: Survey all of the marketing programs and identify the ones that need to be implemented.

Affirmation: The programs I support and manage help the region, branches, and reps make their quotas.

Six-month objective: Introduce a new marketing program that helps double revenue.

Affirmation: My new program has effectively helped the region double its revenue.

One-year objective: Achieve all objectives, thus enabling me to be promoted to marketing manager.

Affirmation: I am a great marketing manager because I put people first.

6. Marketing Manager, $80,000–$90,000   TWO YEARS

One-month objective: Get to know all of my team members and assess their skills, needs, and career objectives.

Affirmation: I am a great marketing manager because I know the needs of my people.

Three-month objective: Have a solid business plan and understanding of how the team unit and branch are going to make their quotas.

Affirmation: I have all of the industry, account, and customer information and resources needed to make quota.

Six-month objective: Double revenue and cut expenses and lead the region in all areas of business measurement.

Affirmation: My team and I are rated number one in the region in all business areas.

One-year objective: Exceed quota by 30 percent and have the highest internal and external opinion survey of any manager in the country.

Affirmation: I work smarter, not harder. I put my people and the customers first. I sincerely go out of my way to do the right thing.

7. Regional Director of Sales, $110,000–$120,000

CREATE A PRIVATE-LIFE GAME PLAN

1. After writing down primary goals for your private life, think about the sort of person you want to be. Where would you like to live? What lifestyle would you like to

have? List step-by-step goals that will help you stretch and grow along the way.

2. Next, list mini-goals that will add value and enrichment to your life, such as increasing levels of fitness, mastery of personal challenges, or courses or experiences that might increase your level of understanding, awareness, or spirituality.

3. Put a deadline on each of them, starting with one month and then going to three months, six months, one year, three years, five years, eight years, and ten years.

4. For each mini-goal, write a positive affirmation stating why the goal is important to you and how it will help you move closer to your primary goal.

Below is a blueprint to assist you in designing your own Private-Life Game Plan.

Shortly after graduating from high school Pat began working full-time in the corporate offices of a major retailer in California. One of her life-long goals is to earn an advanced degree in order to work as a curator at the Smithsonian Institution. She has designed a ten-year life plan that incorporates her four primary goals.

Primary Long-Term Goals:
Earn a bachelor's degree in Art History
Spend quality time with family and friends
Relocate to the Washington, D.C. area
Work as a curator at the Smithsonian

1. YEAR ONE
One-month objective: Talk with Human Resources personnel regarding tuition reimbursement program.
Visit museum and gallery exhibits and lectures at least twice a month.

Reserve one evening per week and one weekend per month for "special" time with family.

Start college selection process.

Affirmation: I am blessed to have the support of my family and supervisor as I resume my education.

Three-month objective: Subscribe to art publications.

Affirmation: I am happy to share my love for art with my family.

Six-month objective: Enroll in speed reading and study skills courses.

Affirmation: I am prepared to return to college after a fifteen year hiatus and continue to work because I know how to maximize my time.

One-year objective: Complete 15 semester units of general education coursework each year at the community college until all 60 units are completed (approximately four years to complete).

1. YEAR THREE

   One-month objective: Volunteer at the local museum to learn more about museum administration and operations.

   Affirmation: I am an enthusiastic volunteer because I am familiar with the exhibitions and all related materials.

   Three-month objective: One week family vacation in Washington, D.C.

   Affirmation: I am able to spend quality time with my family while pursuing my goal to relocate to Washington, D.C.

   Six-month objective: Narrow my decision to three colleges to attend in order to complete undergraduate degree.

   Affirmation: I will select the right college that will provide me with the best learning opportunities.

One-year objective: Internship at an art museum.

Affirmation: I am an enthusiastic intern learning something new everyday that will help with my professional advancement and personal growth.

2. YEAR FIVE

One-month objective: Transfer to four-year college to complete accelerated degree program (18-month program).

Affirmation: I am the best student in my classes because I complete all of the reading assignments and come prepared to discuss the material.

Three-month objective: Create additional study time—5 to 7 A.M. and 9 to 11 P.M. daily.

Affirmation: I am a hard worker and will make time for my educational, family, and professional needs.

Six-month objective: Apply for position at museum.

Affirmation: I am an organized and resourceful administrator who can be depended on to keep abreast of the most recent developments in the field.

One-year objective: One week family vacation in Washington, D.C. to celebrate graduation.

Apply for museum jobs in Washington, D.C. (During years six and seven, Pat and her family relocated to Washington, D.C. where she resumed her studies.)

3. YEAR EIGHT

One-month objective: Completion of master's degree in museum studies.

Affirmation: I will complete my master's degree with honors by studying hard and remaining focused.

Three-month objective: Publication of master's thesis on contemporary West African art.

Affirmation: I will curator a traveling exhibition based on my graduate research.

Six-month objective: Two-week family vacation in Ghana

Affirmation: I am a thoughtful and caring spouse and parent who always makes time for family gatherings.

One-year objective: Purchase home in Silver Spring, Maryland

Affirmation: I will have a beautiful three bedroom home in Silver Spring, Maryland with an affordable mortgage.

4. YEAR TEN

One-month objective: Research project in Senegal and Ivory Coast.

Affirmation: I am chronicling important information for a ground-breaking documentary on an emerging art trend in the region.

Three-month objective: Family to join me for an extended vacation in West Africa.

Affirmation: I am truly blessed to have a loving and supportive family

Six-month objective: Fifth year anniversary at National Museum of African Art.

Enroll in doctoral program in African Studies.

Affirmation: I am an impassioned student of life embracing my intellectual curiosity at every opportunity.

One-year objective: Promotion to Curator for Contemporary African Art.

Affirmation: I will be promoted to curator because of my outstanding research in Senegalese, Ivorian, and Ghanaian art.

I suggest that you reread your game plans at least twice a week as a positive reinforcement. Every time you do that, you implant the goals more deeply into your subconscious mind. Your conscious mind acts upon what your subconscious mind believes.

When you're presented with change, setting goals will make the unfamiliar easier to deal with. But it's important to stay flexible within your plans. Keep in mind that there will be changes within the changes. A friend of mine who works in the infomercial industry says that every decision in her business is "written on sand at low tide." Whatever is decided today will be changed tomorrow, when the tide comes in and wipes the sand clean. Your goals will change as your circumstances change. Flexibility is vital.

In his book *The Wisdom of Your Subconscious Mind*, John K. Williams says there are four powers of the subconscious mind that we must all remember.

- First, you are the architect of your destiny. Every experience in your life—health, illness, poverty, wealth, failure, or success—is the result of actions or purposes you set in motion.
- Second, you have creative power in your life because you can visualize what you want to achieve so clearly that it becomes imprinted on the subconscious mind—which then brings the dream to reality.
- Third, you are a radiating power able to attract to yourself everything you want, providing that you are willing to pay the price.
- Fourth, you are "the building and directing power of your life." There's nothing that is—or that has been—which isn't dependent on the power of the mind. When life presents you with a challenge, it is up to you to meet that challenge. Whether you fail or succeed is up to you and you alone.

Develop a Complete Game Plan

When I first started playing basketball as a boy, I put together a game plan to improve my basketball skills. My first step was to figure out where I was in comparison with other players, where I needed to be, and how to get there. Obviously I needed the benefit of someone else's expertise, a coach who could provide direction and assess my abilities. My dad stepped up and helped me considerably. He preached the virtue of "practice makes for improvement" and found ways to build my confidence and self-esteem as I was learning the fundamentals. He also encouraged me to build the body strength necessary for competitive play so that I was strong enough to be an offensive threat and a tough defender.

One of the interesting things my father did to motivate me was to lower the basketball goal in our driveway from the standard ten feet to eight feet. He noticed that because it was a strain for me to get the ball up to the hoop at the standard height, I was throwing the ball like a shot-putter instead of shooting it. He lowered the hoop to help me develop a better shooting style, and as I grew taller and stronger, he raised it so that I made the adjustment gradually.

My father did the same thing in helping me create a plan to become a better player. He helped me to set small, reachable goals as a defensive move to fend off an attitude of frustration and impatience. As I reached those goals or skill levels, we set new goals. In addition, I began to watch college and pro games to increase my understanding of the sport. It was there that I found my first basketball heroes, who became my goal models. Everyone needs goal models— those who have been down a path similar to the one you hope to take and achieved goals similar to those you've set for yourself. Goal models help you by directing you, by taking you through the steps necessary to realize your dreams.

I followed a growth policy in selecting my basketball goal models. I changed them as I grew, always moving to those players who were my height. When I was six-feet-two-inches tall in the sixth grade, Jerry West was my hero. When I hit six-four, I switched to Pistol Pete Maravich. I studied their moves at the positions they played. It really did help me improve my game.

My goal-modeling wasn't limited to watching the pros play. I also read about them. I wanted to know more than how good they were. I wanted to know how they got that way. Many people study and admire successful people, wanting similar results without understanding their challenges, obstacles, preparation, and the price they had to pay to achieve their success. Once I learned what my goal models did to achieve their level of mastery, I knew what I had to do and the price I had to pay to be successful.

I studied my goal models. I read that when Pistol Pete was developing his game, he treated the basketball like his girlfriend. He gave it a name and took it with him everywhere he went, including to the movies. I called my basketball *Diane*.

Pistol Pete also practiced dribbling and shooting in the gym with the lights out so that he could learn to play by feel and instinct rather than by watching the ball or the hoop. I did the same thing. My mom refers to it as my "Helen Keller" training regimen. Pistol could dribble and shoot equally well with either hand, so I worked on my left-hand coordination. I'd eat, brush my teeth, and comb my hair with my left hand. This will explain to my old classmates why I always had all those food stains on my clothing.

I put a lot into basketball in my teenage years because it was a passion for me, and I had a purpose. I wanted to be a high school All-American, a college All-American, and an NBA All-Star. I had a great attitude while I was working on those goals. In high school, people told me I was too skinny to be any good, but I became an All-American. I think the key to my success was that with my father's help, I had developed an overall game plan with both an offense and a defense geared to keeping my attitude positive and my self-confidence high.

Attitude Tune-Up

- Why was I born? Who am I? What do I want to do with my life starting now? To find my purpose and passion, I need to answer these questions.
- An attitude with purpose and passion is powerful.
- Creating my personal vision helps turn my attitude into action.
- What do I want to do? How am I going to do it? For whom and for what purpose?

There are two great moments in a person's life. The first is when you are born. The second is when you discover why you were born.

—UNKNOWN

CHAPTER SIX

Warning: Attitude Hazards Ahead

STEP 6
Be pre-active.

This step helps you understand the importance of being prepared, never giving up, never quitting, knowing you will overcome. This is the mind-set you need to help you turn attitude into action.

Several years ago, I was invited to be one of the closing speakers for a big IBM rally in San Francisco. There were more than eight hundred people there. I was still working for Big Blue at the time, and I considered it an honor to be invited to address my co-workers, including a group from my hometown, Seattle. I was excited. I wanted, and needed, to be fully prepared. For two and a half weeks I worked on my presentation. I practiced my voice inflections. I worked on my introduction, my main points, the body of my speech, my stories, and my close.

After all that preparation, I was fired up. I scarcely remember the trip from my house to the airport, I was so excited. Once I'd parked the car at the airport garage, I ran to the ticket counter, only to be advised that the flight would be delayed four hours. Now some may have taken that as a negative development. I looked at it as an opportunity to practice for four more hours, and I did, up and down the concourse. Out loud! As I practiced, an older lady approached me and asked, "Sir, excuse me, but to whom are you talking?"

"I'm talking to myself. I'm getting ready for a motivational presentation."

"Well, what I've heard so far sounds really good." It was just the encouragement I needed.

Finally it came time to board the plane. I was seated next to a gentleman who for four and a half hours didn't say a word. He couldn't. I motivated him the whole way. When the plane landed, he jumped up from his seat and gave me a standing ovation. "I've never been on a plane with a motivational speaker, but boy you've got me fired up! You're going to do great!"

I thanked him and hurried off the plane, still fired up. My designated escort met me at the gate. She noticed my enthusiasm immediately and asked how my flight was.

I responded, "Anytime I get from point A to point B, it's always a pretty good flight." She then went on to explain that she had some good news and some bad news.

I asked her two questions, "Am I speaking today? And is the audience breathing?"

She responded yes to both. So I told her, "It all sounds like good news to me. I've been preparing for two weeks, and I'm ready to make a difference."

"I like your attitude," she said. "But we have to move

your speech from one-thirty up to four-thirty. Also, you now have to follow Debbi Fields of Mrs. Field's Cookies, who is one of the top speakers on the circuit. None of the other speakers on the program wanted to follow her. We hope you don't mind."

Still I hung on to my positive attitude. "Let me tell you something. It's been two and a half weeks of preparation, followed by a four-and-a-half-hour flight. I'm so ready I'll follow anybody. And I hope she brought some cookies!"

When we arrived at the ballroom where the conference was being held, Mrs. Fields was concluding her talk. My host asked if I wanted to go in to listen to her closing remarks. I declined, explaining, "I would love to go in and listen to a great speaker like Mrs. Fields, but you have given me a challenge. And I've learned from my grandma that anytime you get a challenge you should break it down to an opportunity. I'm going to stay out in the hallway and practice my speech. I'll know when it's my time to come in."

She said, "Good luck, break a leg."

I didn't know what that meant, but if it was anything good, I was breaking two. I started walking around the hotel lobby talking to myself. *Don't worry about Mrs. Fields. You know what you've got to do.*

All of a sudden, I heard the roar of the crowd. A voice came into my head: *Oh, she's good.* Three minutes later I see two people leaving the ballroom. They're eating chocolate chip cookies. I said to myself, *Oh no, you didn't bring them anything to eat.* Just then a friend came running up and offered these words of encouragement: "I saw your name on the program. Oh Keith, you've got to follow Mrs. Fields? I'll be praying for you because I don't think you can be that good."

My attitude went from an all-time high to a basement-level low in a matter of seconds. My positive internal dialogue automatically switched over to negative. My inner voice said, *Give up. They don't want to hear you speak. They want to go home. You didn't bring them any cookies. In life everyone fails, and today is your turn!*

I believe there is a coach and a spirit that lives within me, and I believe there is a coach and a spirit that lives within you. When times get tough and you're faced with the hazards of life, call on your coach. In the middle of the hotel lobby, I yelled out, "Be quiet! You didn't stay up two and a half weeks and fly four and a half hours to come out here and fail. You'll make a lousy Mrs. Fields, but you can make the best Keith Harrell in the world. You're here to make a difference. Let's go get busy."

I entered the back of the room. I was all prepared to run down the center aisle. The top executive was introducing me, going through my bio. I was so keyed up I was jumping up and down. He kept going on and on with the introduction. My patience ran out. "Hurry up!" I yelled. A woman seated to my right glared up at me. "Oh, *you're* the next speaker. I feel sorry for you. You've got to follow Mrs. Fields and she was *g-o-o-d!*"

I looked down at her with a million dollar smile and said, "Let me tell you something. Don't feel sorry for me. The reason I'm following her is because she can't follow me. You better hang onto your seat and buckle up because I'm going to have an impact!"

I ran down that aisle, jumped up on the stage, and gave my best presentation ever. I had that group so fired up, I had Mrs. Fields baking cookies for me!

Attitude is everything!

Maintaining Control
in Spite of Attitude Hazards

That situation turned out fine, but many times in life it's the hazards of negative comments from others and what we say to ourselves that contribute to our failures, destroying the support we need to stay focused and in control.

You must be clear on your goals and be vigilant about maintaining a positive attitude. When you approach life knowing there are going to be problems, you are able to understand that the problem is not the problem. The "problem" serves as a marker, or an indicator, that allows you to recognize where you are in relation to where you desire to be.

Learning to manage minor hazards is an important step to staying positive. One winter night, I was driving my grandma and my cousin Michael, who happens to be blind, home from Christmas dinner when I heard a thumping noise that sounded like a flat tire. This time I was 100 percent correct. I carefully pulled to the shoulder of the road and got out of the car. As I headed to the trunk, my grandma leaned her head out the window. "Honey, if you need any help let me know. I've changed a few tires in my day, and I still remember how." About this time Michael chimed in, "I can help you, man. Tonight I can see as well as you can out there." I said to myself, *What great attitudes. An eighty-six-year-young grandma and a blind cousin offering their assistance.* They were positive and willing to put their attitudes into action.

We're all faced with life's minor inconveniences and hazards. How much needless energy do you expend on inconsequential matters instead of facing up to the situation and continuing on your journey? I'm reminded of a time when my flight came in unusually late and I was exhausted. All I could think about was getting home. Two weeks earlier, I'd parked my new car in the airport lot and was anxious to get on the highway. When I turned the key in the ignition, nothing happened. The battery was dead. This wasn't what I expected, particularly with a new car, but life is like that too. Unexpected situations occur constantly. Our ability to maneuver through the benign as well as the traumatic changes makes all the difference. If you're constantly stressed by the minor annoyances, chances are you're not going to handle the catastrophic changes well.

Pre-Active Versus Inactive

That's why I believe in being pre-active, being prepared to take action before a situation occurs. Much like taking a test, you know there are certain things you need to do to be well prepared. By being pre-active, you anticipate a situation before it arises. Though I wasn't expecting the battery of my new car to be dead, I did have road service membership, jumper cables in the trunk, and a charged cellular phone handy. By being prepared, I was able to handle the situation with a minimum of stress.

Many of life's catastrophic challenges are definitely beyond our control—tornadoes, earthquakes, hurricanes, the death of a loved one, unexpected illnesses, an unfaithful spouse, and random acts of violence, for example. Though major hazards are beyond our ability to control, they are definitely a part of the human experience, particularly natural disasters. They're inescapable regardless of where you live.

It's been ten years since the Loma Prieta earthquake in San Francisco, and I have a friend who still has a clear image of what happened that day. She told me she was in the middle of hosting a reception for prospective students at the college where she worked when the earthquake struck. It was fifteen seconds of terror. When it was over, sixty-seven people were dead, more than three thousand injured, a major freeway had collapsed, more than a hundred roads were closed, the San Francisco Bay Bridge was broken, and nearly eight thousand more people became homeless that evening.

I'd been in earthquakes before, but this one was different. I knew the drills. I'd heard them all my life: Stand in a doorway. Get under a desk. Have an escape route. Keep an earthquake kit—flashlight, batteries, portable radio, food rations, bottled drinking water. Basically, Keith, I was being what you'd call pre-active. I'd practiced drills in school and even at church. On that day I knew a doorway wouldn't do. With all the talk of the next "big one" I still wasn't prepared.

Unlike a tornado or hurricane, with an earthquake there is no advance warning or mechanism for determining when the hazard is going to occur. Many of life's hazards are the same—disastrous, unpredictable, and beyond your control.

Fear for my life was the motivating factor here. By the time I got everyone out of the building and made it back to my office, the campus seemed deserted. I got in my car and reluctantly headed home. I didn't know what to expect. When I arrived, I found my neighbors standing outside afraid to go in. A gas line had ruptured, and they were waiting for emergency crews to arrive. I went inside to take a quick look at the damage, gather a few belongings, call my parents and a friend to come get me. I was afraid to be alone. While I didn't smell gas, I heard the groans of the building as it shifted. For the next few days, we experienced hundreds of aftershocks.

Whether you go through an earthquake, divorce, or any major catastrophe, you can expect aftershocks. An aftershock is a continued disruption or a major inconvenience that occurs after the initial hazard appears to be over. After an earthquake there's the rebuilding, the insurance to deal with, major detours, and traffic delays. After a divorce, there's the distribution of financial assets, custody issues, and emotional challenges.

My home had always been a place where I felt safe, but hazards have a way of making familiar and trusted places seem unstable and unaccommodating. I stayed with friends for two nights. At the end of the week, I returned to work, even though there wasn't much to do since our offices were being relocated across campus. Just being among my colleagues and the students was comforting. On my way home from work I stopped by a store to replenish my earthquake kit—batteries for my flashlight and radio, bottled water, supplies for my first-aid kit. I withdrew emergency money from the ATM and invested in a cell phone. I decided to be as prepared as possible for the next one.

Catastrophic life hazards have a way of throwing you completely off balance. When devastation hits and you feel as if your life is no longer yours to control, it's important to reestablish a routine. This could be something as basic as getting up at the same time each day and having a set time to meditate or pray or eat. The shock may linger, the memory certainly doesn't go away, but you can adapt and eventually recover. How well you recover from life's earthquakes and hurricanes determines your ability to handle the next aftershock or storm.

Let's look at what my friend did to take control of the disastrous situation:

1. Used fear as a motivator and took action
2. Supported other people in a crisis situation
3. Shared her concern with others
4. Monitored her inner dialogue
5. Became pre-active by planning for the next hazard
6. Sought support from others
7. Maintained a routine that helped keep her attitude in action

Facing the Hazard of Fear

Whether the hazard is major or minor, expected or unexpected, what normally surfaces and hinders our ability to take action is fear. A woman shared her story with me about the hazards of flying:

I'd been back East for a number of meetings and a conference. The day I was to travel from Boston to New York, I couldn't decide whether I wanted to drive or fly. I returned the rental car and went to my gate to discover the flight was indefinitely delayed. With each passing hour, I told myself there wasn't anything to worry about, probably just my usual anxiety about flying. It didn't help at all when the plane finally arrived. It was one of those small twelve-seater commuter planes. I definitely didn't want to board, but forced myself at the last minute. I hated flying, yet I'd accepted a job that required me to travel four months out of the year. I've always believed in facing my fears.

Years earlier, I'd actually undergone hypnosis to see if it would help. It did for a while, but the fear never completely vanished.

I struck up a conversation with the woman seated across the aisle from me. I was barely buckled in when somehow I managed to tell her about my fear of flying. She reassured me that everything would be fine. She said she frequently took the short flight into Manhattan. Plus, her husband was a pilot and had flown the same type of plane. She seemed to know the safety record and it was good. I looked around and everyone seemed calm except for me. I told myself to stop stressing. *In a few short hours you'll be in New York trying on shoes.* I said my prayers and readjusted my seat belt.

About twenty to twenty-five minutes into our flight we all realized something was wrong. All conversations stopped. The plane didn't seem to be responding as it should. It suddenly lost altitude. We started a rapid descent. People started screaming. The man in the seat in front of me threw up. The woman in the aisle across from me grabbed my hand and started praying. The plane was still dropping. Time stopped. Somehow the pilot managed to level off, but there was obviously a mechanical problem. As he struggled to keep the plane airborne, a sense of dread overtook the cabin. My companion and I continued to hold hands and pray. As we approached JFK, I looked out the window and saw the fire trucks lined up on the runway. As scared as I was, I knew I'd survive and prayed that the pilot's will to live was as strong as mine. It was a rough landing, but we were all fine. Traumatized, but fine. As we all hugged and cried tears of relief, I managed to regain my composure, claim my luggage, and hail a taxi to my hotel.

I was a grateful wreck. It was an unexpected hazard, one that I was able to walk away from, but I knew in three short days I had to get back on a plane and make the five-hour flight home. All my old fears resurfaced. I had a choice to make. How was I going to get back to California? More important, how was I going to keep my job if I was too afraid to fly? Fortunately, I was meeting friends, and they managed to calm my frayed nerves. They gave me the pep talk I needed and convinced me of the impracticality of taking the train back to California. Through the help of friends, a major attitude adjustment, and trusting in my faith, I was well on my way to overcoming my fear of flying.

How did this person take control of a disaster?

1. Sought help for her fear
2. Exercised her faith through prayer
3. Shared her concern with others
4. Monitored her inner dialogue

Keeping Your Faith

When you put your attitude into action, you start to overcome the hazards you're facing. Once you accept that there are going to be hazards and challenges in life, you're better prepared and able to adjust your attitude, do what you need to do to take action, and then start rejoicing, because you know your victory is on the other side. When you go through problems or hazards, have faith.

It's important to walk by faith, not by sight. Remember, don't let your vision fool you, because you may look around and see that things are not immediately getting better. This is where faith comes in. Faith is the evidence of things not seen but hoped for.

When you are in the midst of hard times, and negative things are happening, remain faithful. Know that the circumstance is temporary, so don't worry.

Victory Lies on the Other Side of Each Challenge

I've heard it reported that some people spend upwards of 92 percent of their time worrying for no good reason. You can't get through life without experiencing some type of hazard, but worrying about what lies ahead is foolish. Although there are going to be problems, remember, your victory is on the other side.

I was cruising along, a few years back, filled with purpose, passion, and a positive attitude. Then I got blind-sided. I noticed strange swellings in both lower legs. I was supposed to catch a flight to Los Angeles to speak to employees of the Mattel Corporation, but I decided to make a quick trip to the doctor's office first. When the doctor examined my legs, he calmly offered his diagnosis: blood clots in both legs.

Initially I looked at this as a minor challenge. I asked the doctor to write a prescription because I had a plane to catch. That's when he told me that it was a far more serious problem than I'd realized. "If you move too quickly, and one of those blood clots releases and goes up to your heart, you won't have to worry about your flight, your speaking engagement, or anything else," he said.

My attitude adjusted immediately. I called my contacts at Mattel and told them we would have to reschedule. I then went straight from the doctor's office to the hospital, where I stayed on my back for two weeks to prevent the clots from moving into an artery. There were plenty of opportunities to let my attitude slide into self-pity and frustration, but I chose to be thankful that I'd gone to a doctor who identified the problem.

Sooner or later, we all get hit with challenges that set off the Attitude Hazard alarms. A loved one becomes ill or gets injured, a shift in technology threatens your work, a sudden change in the weather turns a routine trip into a test of survival. Stuff happens! You can't spend your life hiding behind your fears, worries, or self-doubt.

So what do you do? How do you prepare yourself to deal with things that you can't control? By focusing on those things that you can control, and by being determined to get a positive result out of even the most negative experience. Whenever you undertake a new endeavor, it's important to know the rules of the game. Whether it's a new job, a new relationship, or a new challenge, there's a process you must go through in order to learn the rules. As this learning process unfolds, we encounter problems and complexities that can easily give rise to additional Attitude Hazards, including:

- Self-doubt. *I don't know if I can really do this. It's more complicated than I thought.*
- Frustration. *Why isn't this working? What am I doing wrong?*
- Fear of failure. *If I don't figure this out, I'm in trouble. They'll kick me off the team.*
- Anxiety. *This is my one chance and I'm blowing it.*
- Anger. *Leave me alone! You're so stupid!*
- Victimization. *Why me? Nobody cares what happens to me. Why am I singled out?*
- Blame. *It's all your fault.*

Response Versus Reaction

It's amazing how quickly a positive attitude can be shut down by a few bad experiences and negative thoughts, isn't it? That's why it's so important to monitor your attitude and respond rather than react.

When you *respond*, you make a positive and constructive mental adjustment. When you *react,* it's purely emotional and rarely does anything to improve the situation; often it makes it worse. That's why they have Emergency *Response* Teams, not Emergency *Reaction* Teams. If your doctor has prescribed a medication and told you to come back in two weeks, wouldn't you rather hear him say that your body is *responding* to the treatment rather than *reacting* to it?

Still not clear on the distinction? Let's say you've just received word that you're going to be downsized in six weeks.

A reaction would be *I'm losing my job and my source of income. This is going to devastate my family and throw us for a loop.*

A response would be *I'd better get the résumé updated, contact a headhunter, and begin exploring my options.*

When you simply react, you go with your gut emotional instinct, with little thought of the long-range consequences. When you respond, your brain is fully engaged and your self-awareness is high. You have the long-term big picture in mind.

Negative thoughts are going to creep into your mind. The key is to be prepared with a game plan that responds offensively and defensively rather than one that merely reacts. Choosing to respond instead of reacting helps you stay in control of your attitude and your life. It's the difference between having an attitude that sends you flying out the door eager and excited each morning and having an attitude that keeps you under the covers hitting the snooze alarm.

Remember, hazards come in all shapes and sizes, designed to set you back, knock you down, or destroy you. In life there are going to be challenges. Stay positive, have a solid plan, take action, and you will be equipped to face all of life's challenges. Keep your faith!

Attitude Tune-Up

- Watch out for negative inputs. The loudest voice you hear is your own.
- Maintain control in spite of the hazards of life.
- Learn to respond rather than react.
- The problem is not the problem. Your victory is on the other side.
- Don't worry about what you can't control. Remember, 92 percent of your worries are for no good reason.
- Have a plan. Be pre-active rather than inactive.
- Conquer fear by taking action.

Fear cannot scare a person who is at peace with God. There is no room, opportunity, or place for fear in such a person. Remember, you must have faith.

CHAPTER SEVEN

Your Attitude Tool Kit

STEP 7

Discover how to motivate yourself.

This step supplies the energy and enthusiasm to keep you going. You will acquire the tools to jump-start yourself and help turn your attitude into action.

On my first day in junior high, my homeroom teacher handed me a note telling me I had to go to speech therapy class. I was shocked. For most of my life my family had been telling me that I would outgrow my stutter, just as one of my uncles had outgrown his. I'd shot up four inches during summer break, and none of my clothes fit. I'd attended speech therapy all summer, and my stuttering had decreased significantly. Based on all that evidence, I was sure that I'd outgrown the school's speech therapy program.

I disliked speech therapy class because it made me feel different. Every year in school up to that point, I'd had to leave my classmates two days a week for the special training.

They knew I had a problem. They'd heard me suffer through enough readings. I didn't want to make it any more obvious than I had to.

My teacher, Mr. Brown, was cool. He didn't make the announcement in front of my new classmates. He came to me and told me quietly. I told Mr. Brown that I didn't need speech class anymore. He insisted that I go. I assured him that I would be right back because there must have been a mistake.

Reach into the Attitude Tool Kit

On the way down to the speech therapy class, I gave myself a pep talk. *I'm not going to stutter anymore. I'm through with it. I speak clearly now. I'm not going to stutter anymore. I'm through with it. I speak clearly now.* I didn't think of the words I said as affirmations, but looking back, they fit the definition of a tool used for self-motivation. And they worked.

I was still repeating my affirmation as I walked into the room and up to the therapist, who was standing at the front of the class. My heart was racing, but my focus was intense. I looked the therapist in the eye and started talking faster—and more clearly—than I ever had in my life: "I'm Keith Harrell, and they told me to come here for help. But I've been in speech therapy for six years now, and I've practiced my therapy from my old instructor all summer, and I don't stutter anymore. I've outgrown it. My grandma told me that the day would come when I would outgrow it and that day is here!"

When I finished my little speech, the instructor looked at me with a mixture of kindness and confusion. "I do have you on my list for therapy, Keith, but you're right. It sounds like you don't need it anymore," he said.

At first I was confused. Then it hit me. I had gotten through that entire speech without stuttering! I was so focused on the words, I didn't pay any attention to the delivery.

"That was great, Keith. Now I'd like you to read something for the class. If you can do that, we'll know for sure that you've outgrown your stutter. It will inspire the other kids. I'm going to introduce you to them now," he said.

"Class, hard work is going to pay off for you. Keith stuttered, and for six years he went to speech twice a week. He worked all summer, and he says that he doesn't stutter anymore. I've asked him to read to you so you can see how well he has done."

The entire time the therapist was talking, I was repeating my affirmation.

"Keith? Are you ready?"

I focused on the words on the page of the book he'd handed me, and I began reading. The words flowed out of my mouth. The kids in the classroom leaned forward in their chairs. Many of them had known me for a long time. They'd never heard me talk so clearly. My confidence grew as I read. For the first time, the other kids weren't snickering or laughing at me. Some were cheering me on, because if I could do it, they felt they could too.

I had never before dared to look up from a page while I was reading aloud, but I did that day. I even threw in a few dramatic effects as I completed the story. I felt like an actor delivering an Academy Award–winning performance. There was applause when I finished. You can be sure I took a little bow too.

I was excited, but so was everyone else. "You don't have to come to speech class anymore, Keith," the teacher said. "I'm proud of you. We're all proud of you. Would you come back sometime and read to us again?"

I told him I'd be glad to. Then I ran out of the speech therapy room and headed straight for the school office. I was so excited I couldn't wait to call my mom.

As soon as she said, "This is Florence Harrell," I said, "Mmmn, Mmmm, Mmmm, Mmm, I don't have to go to speech anymore!"

"Slow down, slow down," she said. "You're stuttering, honey."

"No, no, I'm not stuttering. I'm just excited, Mom, because I don't stutter anymore. I've grown out of it!"

I'd grown out of stuttering, and I'd grown out of my fearful attitude when it came to speaking in front of other people. I'd also grown out of any sense of being victimized by my speech impediment. That day I learned the power of affirmations, which are Tool 1 in your Attitude Tool Kit. Affirmations are statements of faith in our dreams, goals, and ability to take control of our lives. They are part of an array of helpful tools you can use to help you focus, build confidence, and eliminate self-doubt, fears, and other counterproductive thoughts. Other attitude tools include self-motivation, visualization, attitude talk, powerful greetings, enthusiasm, spiritual empowerment, humor, and exercise.

Attitude Tool 1
Self-Coaching Through Affirmations

Affirmations repeated several times each day, every day, serve to reprogram your subconscious with positive thinking. An affirmation is made up of words—words charged with power, conviction, and faith. Every time you speak, atoms of your body are affected; their rate of vibration is either raised or lowered. This process involves repetition, feeling, and imagining.

An affirmation is a method for affirming something positive in your mind. It may involve stating something that you think to be true even when all evidence appears to be to the contrary. An affirmation contains the elements of your belief, attitude, and motivation.

You send a positive response to your subconscious, which accepts whatever you tell it. When done properly, this triggers positive feelings that, in turn, drive action. Imagining is the process that allows you to see the affirmation in your mind. Once you can see it in your mind, you'll be closer to achieving it in your life.

Affirmations not only help to keep you positive, they also stir the power within you. This power needs to be coached and guided to maximize your performance.

One of my favorite affirmations is by Pastor Chuck Swindoll. It's called "Attitudes"—and it goes like this:

ATTITUDES

Words can never adequately convey the incredible impact of our attitude toward life. The longer I live the more convinced I become that life is 10 percent what happens to us and 90 percent how we respond to it.

I believe the single most significant decision I can make on a day-to-day basis is my choice of attitude. It is more important than my past, my education, my bankroll, my successes or failures, fame or pain, what other people think of me or say about me, my circumstances, or my position. Attitude keeps me going or cripples my progress. It alone fuels my fire or assaults my hope. When my attitudes are right, there's no barrier too high, no valley too deep, no dream too extreme, no challenge too great for me.

Learning to craft a custom-made affirmation can be a powerful tool in helping you create a positive attitude and transform it into positive actions. The statements you design for your affirmations must be positive and in the present or future tense. An affirmation is something you say to take control of your thoughts, emotions, and attitudes. To work well, it should have these five attributes:

1. Be uniquely yours
2. Be uplifting
3. Deal with what is going on at that moment
4. Paint a picture in your mind
5. Touch your heart

Avoid using tenuous words such as *try, wish,* or *hope* in your affirmations. You want a statement that has the ring of an established truth, not a desire. "I am somebody!" has a lot more power than "I'm trying to be somebody!"

Look at this list of five events that might cause you to develop a bad attitude. Try to come up with at least one positive affirmation for each on your own. I've included my own examples to help you.

1. After thirteen years, your job has been eliminated, and you are downsized.
   • *With my network of professional contacts, I will be able to make a smooth transition to another position.*
2. Your doctor restricts you to bed rest for two weeks.
   • *I can take this opportunity to write and review my goals.*
   • *I can begin or finish reading my personal development books.*
3. Your flight has been canceled because of equipment failure.
   • *I'm glad the problem was detected before we were airborne.*
   • *The flying conditions may be better later.*

4. Your property taxes go up 15 percent.
   - *This will mean more funding to improve our schools.*
   - *The value of my home has increased, meaning that it's a better investment than I thought.*
5. Your doctor has detected a blockage in one of your arteries.
   - *The early detection probably saved my life.*
   - *This is a wake-up call to start taking better care of myself.*

Now take a look at the affirmations I have provided and the ones you came up with. Most of them not only reflect a positive attitude but also offer a course of action. They give you something to visualize.

For many years, the young fighter Muhammad Ali told everyone "I'm the greatest!" Today, few people would disagree that he was the greatest of his day and is one of the greatest in boxing history.

In the 1993–94 season, the Houston Rockets were struggling in the NBA playoffs. When they walked onto their home court and saw huge banners carrying the affirmation "We believe," it helped inspire and motivate the players. Assured that they were not in it alone, that their fans and their city were behind them, the Rockets went on to win the championship that year, and the next year too. I'm sure that Akeem Olajuwon and his teammates had something to do with it too, but there's no doubt that when the fans told the players "We believe," the players began to believe more in themselves, just as the Dallas Cowboys pumped up their attitudes for years as "America's Team."

Affirmations are such a big part of sports that we hardly notice them. What could be a more classic affirmation than the old cheerleading chant that goes "S-U-C-C-E-S-S. *That's the way we spell success!*" Sports marketing has long embraced affirmations as a way to pitch products. Nike's *"Just Do It!"*

started out as an ad slogan and became a favorite affirmation of teams and athletes around the world.

Attitude Tool 2
Self-Motivation Through Discovering Your Motives

The first step in motivating yourself is to discover a motive that moves you. The dictionary defines *motive* as "that which incites a person to take action." A motive helps you take action to change your life. Basic motives for action include love, self-preservation, anger, financial gain, and fear. The three strongest are love, fear, and financial gain.

Brenda, a young single mother, used fear and love to help her daughter. In the process, she overcame a childhood phobia and discovered an unlikely passion and a new career. Brenda had always had trouble keeping up in school, and her weakest subject was always math. She enrolled in a remedial mathematics course at the local community college because she loved her daughter and feared she wouldn't be able to assist her with her homework. She earned an A in the course, which inspired her to set a higher goal. She decided to earn her college degree.

"My earliest memory of school is being told I was stupid. It was in the third grade. I'd recently transferred into the class," she recalled. "There was a problem on the blackboard, and I raised my hand. When I answered incorrectly, the teacher called me stupid. All the kids laughed. I just hung my head and fought back the tears. I always felt I wasn't smart enough. I always feared I would end up a failure because I felt I wasn't very bright."

After barely graduating from high school, she worked at several low-paying, dead-end jobs and was barely getting by.

Things changed after her daughter was born. She became highly motivated to set an example and to build a better life for the two of them. Knowing her options were limited without a degree, she returned to school and graduated with a degree in computer science. Brenda now works at a high-tech firm and tutors students in advanced mathematics. Because of her love for her daughter, Brenda put her attitude into action, overcame her fear of failure, and created a better life for her family.

I recently encountered someone who had learned to become his own master motivator by discovering his motives. I'd just taken my seat on a flight when the fellow next to me introduced himself and made the standard inquiry: "What do you do for a living?"

"I'm a motivational speaker and consultant. What do you do?"

"I sell pickles," he said. "Do you know anything about pickles? Nobody sells pickles like I sell pickles. I love pickles! Did you know that the pickle comes from the cucumber family? There are hundreds of different kinds of pickles. There's sweet, dill, sour, crispy, chopped, diced, relish, pickle juice, all kinds of pickles. You can eat pickles with everything any time of day. I love pickles. I have some pickles in my bag. I don't think we're going to have a meal on this flight, but if you get tired of eating pretzels, I can make you a pickle sandwich."

At that time, the flight attendant asked if we wanted a beverage and he started asking her if she would like some pickles and if she thought anybody on the plane might want some. He had plenty for everyone.

When he took a breath, I asked him how he developed this pickle passion.

"I used to have a job in a different business altogether and I got laid off. I saw an ad in the classifieds calling for salespeople to sell pickles. I didn't really know a lot about pickles, but I needed a job. At first, when I'd meet people like you on the road and they'd ask me what I did for a living, I'd just tell them I was in the food business. I was a little embarrassed telling people I sold pickles. But one day I realized that by selling pickles, I'd been given a new quality of life. My wife is happy. We have a nice home, a nice car, and the opportunity to be active in our community. I have a little boy who's sick, but thanks to the fact that people are buying my pickles, my wife can stay home and take care of him. I love pickles. Don't forget, if you need some pickles I can get you some. If anybody you know needs some pickles, call me and I'll take care of them."

The plane landed, and as we got off we shook hands and he handed me his business card. On the front of it was a big green pickle. I keep it in my wallet as a reminder of someone who understands the importance of self-motivation. The underlying motive is his love for his family. It's important to discover what motivates you in order to have the passion you need to achieve your success.

Remember, the strongest form of motivation is internal. Motivation is not permanent. You need to do something every day to maintain your energy, focus, and enthusiasm.

The danger of relying on outside motivation is that it's like listening to a John Phillips Sousa march. While it's playing, the music will really get you on your feet, but once the music stops you're likely to sit back down and wait for the next song. I want you to be able to keep on dancing long after I stop banging the drums.

The Art and Science of Human Motivation
Since people have different needs and different desires, they're motivated in many different ways. When someone is

powerfully motivated, it's usually to fulfill a very strong need. Human motivation is a complex field that has been studied extensively by psychologists, behaviorists, and philosophers. Scientists have employed everything from electricity to chemicals that stimulate specific areas of the human brain to determine what motivates us.

The late Abraham Maslow, a psychologist and philosopher who pioneered our understanding of human motivation, is best known for his self-actualization theory. This theory holds that each of us has a hierarchy of needs that must be satisfied, ranging from basic physiological requirements like air, food, and water to emotional needs such as love, esteem, and, finally, self-fulfillment.

Maslow believed that as each level of need is met, we move on to the next higher level. If the most primary needs aren't met, we have to stay focused on fulfilling those needs. If, for example, you are constantly cold and hungry, you are unlikely to be concerned about whether you are intellectually stimulated. After the primary needs for survival are met, Maslow believed our next priority to be personal safety, followed by social interaction, and then self-worth, self-esteem, status, and recognition. Last, but not least, is the need for self-actualization, or self-fulfillment—the need to realize our full purpose and potential. "A musician must make music, an artist must paint, a poet must write, if he is to be ultimately at peace with himself. What a man can be, he must be," Maslow wrote.

Motivation is the hope that puts attitude into action in an attempt to fulfill a desire or achieve a specific result. Self-motivation requires at least these five qualities:

1. *Enthusiasm.* To stay motivated, you've got to have goals that excite you and a plan that gives you instant feedback.

2. *A positive outlook.* Even when your circumstances may not be the best, you have to look on the positive side to stay motivated, because your subconscious mind accepts the information you give it.

3. *A positive physiology.* Changing your physiology can help change your attitude. Notice how differently you feel when you smile, sit up straight, hold your head up high, or walk with purpose. Try walking 25 percent faster and you'll begin to feel and look as if you have a purpose.

4. *Positive memories.* Good memories are money in the bank when it comes to shifting from a negative attitude to a positive one. When you're feeling down and out, you can always tap into a memory that reminds you how good life can be. I suggest that you help build up your positive memory bank by putting together a Win Book, where you put all of the positive notes, e-mails, and other things you receive from people. It's a book or journal where you can record the positive events and experiences in your life. Don't forget to write positive letters to other people so they can build their own positive motivation based on your feedback. You'll find it improves your attitude, because what goes around comes around.

5. *A belief in yourself and your God-given potential.* This is why it is so important to take time to identify the talents, skills, and knowledge that make you a unique person with unlimited potential. When you know and believe in your uniqueness, you want to develop those talents and see them manifest.

Attitude Tool 3
The Power of Visualization

Modern studies of the psychology of peak performance have found that most great athletes, surgeons, engineers, and artists use affirmations and visualizations either subconsciously or consciously to enhance and focus their skills.

Dr. Maxwell Maltz, a reconstructive and cosmetic facial surgeon, wrote one of the first books that established the true power of visualization in controlling and maintaining a positive attitude. He was sixty-one years old when he wrote the classic self-help book *Psycho-Cybernetics* in 1960. He realized that a great many of the patients who had come to him so that they could look better were still insecure and unhappy even with their "perfect" faces. He understood that visualization was a powerful method for self-therapy.

In *Psycho-Cybernetics*, Maltz tells of a visualization experiment he conducted with a basketball team. He had five team members practice shooting foul shots in the gym for several days. Five others practiced shooting only in their minds, visualizing themselves shooting free throws and making each shot. After the five practice days, Maltz staged a contest between the two teams. The players who had visualized themselves making free throws did much better than those who had actually done it.

Today, more and more amateur and professional athletes are spending considerable time on their *mental* training. Pole-vaulters use visualization to see themselves progress through every step of their jumps. They not only visualize their goals, they also imagine exactly what their bodies feel like when they make perfect vaults. Research shows we learn faster with this type of mental visualization. Sports psychologists say that such mental training sends neuromuscular signals that lead to a stronger, more effective performance during the actual event or game.

Phil Jackson, former coach of the Chicago Bulls and now with the Los Angeles Lakers, is a big believer in the power of visualization. In his book, *Sacred Hoops*, Jackson notes that he encourages his players to use visualization to calm themselves during time-outs in games. He advises them to think of a "safe spot" where they feel secure as a method for taking a "short mental vacation" before he gives them directions.

Jackson said that several of his players practice visualization before games, thinking about what's going to happen and how they will react to it. Players say that pregame visualization exercises help them react more quickly in game situations. The coach said he generally does forty-five minutes of visualization at home before each game to prepare his mind and to come up with last-minute adjustments. Jackson uses visualization "to link the grand vision of the team I conjure up every summer to the evolving reality on the court. That vision becomes a working sketch that I adjust, refine and sometimes scrap altogether as the season develops." He also uses visualization to calm himself and to detach himself emotionally from the game because in his early years of coaching he had a tendency to argue a lot with the referees, which resulted in the team being penalized.

Nelson Mandela has written extensively on how visualization helped him maintain a positive attitude while being imprisoned for twenty-seven years. "I thought continually of the day when I would walk free. Over and over, I fantasized about what I would like to do," he wrote in his autobiography.

Visualization works well with affirmations to improve your attitude and self-motivation.

It's strange that we don't feel odd or self-conscious using the same tools for developing a negative attitude. How many times have you visualized yourself failing and then gone out and done it? How many negative messages do you send yourself every day? *What a dumb mistake! I'm not smart enough for the job. I knew I wasn't good enough to get the promotion. I'll always be a C student.*

It takes the same amount of effort to create positive visualizations and affirmations as to create negative ones, but the positive motivational tools will move you forward, and the negative will hold you back.

Attitude Tool 4
Attitude Talk for Positive Internal Dialogue

Positive internal dialogue is what I refer to as "attitude talk." I recommend attitude talk as a way to override your past negative programming by erasing or replacing it with a conscious positive internal voice that helps you face new directions. Your internal conversation—that little voice you listen to all day long—acts like a seed in that it programs your brain and affects your behavior. Fortunately, the information in our brains can be reprogrammed. We have the choice to take a closer look at what we're saying to ourselves and start reprogramming for personal and professional success.

Attitude talk differs from affirmations in that attitude talk can only be heard by you, while affirmations are positive statements spoken out loud with power and conviction.

Consider three of the most common influences that can program us daily and that have the potential for a positive or negative impact on our internal dialogue:

1. *Television.* With all the violence on television today, it's no wonder crime and violence in some areas of the country

are higher than ever before. On the other hand, educational, spiritual, sports, and comedy programs focus more on the importance of positive values. Start monitoring what you watch on television.

Studies show that the subconscious mind is at its most receptive five minutes before we doze off at night. This period is when the mind also reviews events, experiences, and thoughts that occurred to us that day. Typically, we review the negative stories. We also might watch the late news as we doze off. Talk about negative influences: murders, wars, family violence, baseball strikes. No wonder we sometimes wake up in an agitated state of mind. Turn off the television before bed!

2. *Newspapers.* Many people program themselves every morning or every evening by reading a newspaper, which contain both positive and negative articles. Make a habit of finishing your paper by finding a positive story to program your attitude and your inner dialogue. I'd suggest that you not read the newspaper first thing in the morning. Save that for later. Instead, feed your attitude some positive thoughts at that hour. It's better for your attitude and your self-motivation to take a moment to be thankful for being blessed with another day before you read about the latest tragedies that often occupy the front pages of our local and national papers.

3. *Other people.* What other people say and do greatly influence us and our inner thoughts. It's important to filter out negative comments or actions.

Below are some examples of negative internal dialogues. As you read them, compare them with your own conversations and add your own phrases to the list.

NEGATIVE INTERNAL DIALOGUE

- I just know it won't work.
- I hate my job and the people I work with.
- I'm not artistic.
- I'm too old to do anything else in life.
- I just don't have the energy to make a change.
- I ought to take care of it now, but it'll wait until tomorrow.
- Nothing ever seems to go right for me.
- I will start my diet tomorrow.
- If it weren't for bad luck, I wouldn't have any luck at all.
- I'm at the end of my rope.
- If only I were smarter.
- Mondays are not good days for me.

EXAMPLES OF ATTITUDE TALK

- I know it will work because I'll put all of my effort into making this a success.
- With all the people out of work today, I am blessed to have a job.
- I am creative in my own way.
- Age is only a number, and the number I carry today is Number One.
- I have been storing my energy, and I'm now ready to handle change.
- Tomorrow is not guaranteed. I won't put off until tomorrow what I can do today.
- Today I will be judged by my effort and my positive attitude, which will ensure that every day is a super-fantastic day.
- I feel better about myself today because I know the importance of a healthy diet.
- I can be the best me in the world.

- I live my life by having faith, persistence, and a positive attitude.
- Today is the first day of the rest of my life. I am enhancing my skills daily.
- Every day is an opportunity—I can't get to Friday until I step on Monday.

Start listening to your internal voice. Every day, write down your internal conversation, both positive and negative. This exercise will help you gain control over the words that affect your attitude.

Attitude Tool 5
The Power in a Positive Greeting

There is a power in the words that we use, the things that we say, and the things that we do. That's why I advise you to use words that lift up your attitude and the attitudes of those around you. Most people greet each other with words that have no power or energy. For example, when asked how we are doing or how we feel, some average responses are "I'm OK," "I guess I'm making it," "I'll survive," "I'm hangin' in," "Is it payday?" "I don't know right now, talk to me later." One of my favorite responses was from a man I met in a lobby of a hotel. When I asked how he was doing, he responded, "I'm just getting out from under things." Having some fun with this person, I said, "With that attitude, looks like you need to go back!"

He laughed and said, "You're probably right!"

You can have a positive and lasting impact on another person's life with small gestures of thoughtfulness or a few encouraging words. I was alone in an airport terminal somewhere in the wee hours of the morning waiting for a connecting flight when I heard someone whistling a cheerful tune that lightened my mood. I looked up to see that the happy whistler was a cleaning lady emptying trash cans. She looked to be near retirement age, if not older. I smiled and asked her how she was feeling.

"Brand new!" she said enthusiastically. "Every day I wake up is a brand new day for me, and for you too."

I was struck by her level of enthusiasm so early in the morning, and also by her obvious sense of pride in the job she was doing. I have no doubt that she was feeling brand new because of her positive approach to life. She brightened my day simply with a positive greeting.

I try to spread the cheer too, by offering my own version of the cleaning lady's "brand new" line. When folks ask me how I'm doing, I say "Super-fantastic!"

One important secret to internal motivation and being positive: When you're feeling somewhat down-spirited, don't tell people how you feel, *tell them how you want to feel.* By controlling what you say, using positive words with enthusiasm, you help to change your physical and mental state. Not only are the benefits self-rewarding, but you'll recognize the positive impact you have on others.

While working at IBM, every time someone walked by my office and greeted me, I would respond with a big positive "I feel super-fantastic!" It wasn't long before people started to ask how I felt just to hear if I would say something else. It became so popular that if I accidentally said, "I feel great!" people would be disappointed and ask if everything was OK.

Most people enjoy working and living with people who try to view life, and live life, for what it is—a beautiful gift. I'll never forget the person in my audience who, hearing my talk on using positive responses, came up to me after my presentation. He said, "Sir, I don't mean to sound negative—" and I thought to myself, *Well, don't.* He then said, "—but how can you tell people that you feel super-fantastic every day? That's impossible!" I looked at him with a big smile and said, "I don't have to feel super-fantastic every day. All I have to do is feel it today! The key is, if you don't feel it, you tell people how you want to feel, and it won't be long before you do." The person smiled and said, "I think I got it."

Attitude Tool 6
Enthusiasm, a Vital Tool for Staying Motivated

Enthusiasm is another vital tool for maintaining a positive attitude and for staying motivated. Enthusiasm is to attitude what breathing is to life. Enthusiasm enables you to apply your gifts more effectively. It engages the spirit that moves within. The English word *enthusiasm* is derived from the Greek *enthousiasmos*, which means "inspiration." The two root words are *enthous* and *entheos*, which mean "God or spirit within."

When I talk about enthusiasm in my seminars, I ask my audience three questions: Where do you buy it? How do you get it? How much does it cost? I then do an exercise in which I divide the attendees into two or three groups, depending on the audience size. I challenge them to make noise, to let it go, to let out all of their enthusiasm for a full five seconds.

I turn this into a contest, telling them the loudest group will get a prize. What group do you think makes the most noise? The last group. It never fails. If there are three groups, the second group does slightly better than the first, but the last group always uses every ounce of its collective enthusiasm to give an outstanding effort.

Why is it that adults wait to compete before giving their best? After the exercise, most adults want another chance, which lets me remind them of the old adage that you never get a second chance to make a first impression. When I give this same exercise to children, there is no differentiation between groups. What group would you say wins? They all do. The first group is just as loud as the last group. Children don't care who is watching. They love a challenge; they love to let go.

My friend Dr. Metcalf views enthusiasm as "sharing what you have inside yourself with others." For me, enthusiasm is an internal spirit that speaks through your actions from your commitment and your belief in what you are doing. Enthusiasm means putting yourself in motion. In my speeches and seminars, I ask thousands of people each year "How many people like a person who demonstrates sincere, honest enthusiasm?" From the responses I receive, there is no doubt that enthusiasm is one of the most empowering and attractive characteristics you can have.

- Enthusiasm gives you the power to get up early when you are not a morning person.
- Enthusiasm keeps you working on a project instead of quitting.
- Enthusiasm gives you the courage to take the risks needed for success.
- Enthusiasm fuels motivation to make things happen.
- Enthusiasm brightens your personality.
- Enthusiasm combats fear and worry.
- Enthusiasm distinguishes a championship team from an average team.

- Enthusiasm is the fire in the belly that says, "Don't wait!"
- Enthusiasm is the burning desire that communicates commitment, determination, and spirit. It shows everyone else that you are sold on what you are doing and that you are seriously motivated.
- Enthusiasm's last four letters stand for I Am Seriously Motivated.
- Enthusiasm and a positive attitude are the winning ingredients for success.

Attitude Tool 7
Connecting to Your Spiritual Empowerment

The ultimate level of human need extends into the spiritual realm. Just as we feed our bodies in response to our primary need to survive physically, we need to feed our spirit because we are spiritual beings. I reached this conclusion by reading one of the first and most successful motivational tools of all time, the Bible. A great deal of the self-help and motivational material available today springs from this source. In fact, I've been told that the word *BIBLE* is really an acronym that stands for Basic Instructions Before Leaving Earth.

The Bible, a global best-seller, includes these powerful words:

I will never leave you, nor forsake you.

—JOSHUA 1:5

All things are possible to him that believes.

—MARK 9:23

Walk by faith, not by sight.

—2 CORINTHIANS 5:7

The Lord is on my side; I will fear not: what can man do unto me?

—PSALMS 118:6

Many people find powerful and positive motivation in their faith. I happen to be one of them. I've referred to the Bible to make the point that self-motivation is a serious and deeply rooted part of human existence. All of the well-known affirmations and positive motivational tools of today sprang from the Bible.

Attitude Tool 8
Lighten Up Your Life with Humor

Humor is a powerful motivator. The more humor and laughter in your life, the less stress you'll have, which in turn means more positive energy to help you put your attitude into action.

While working at IBM, a company that at least back then was known for being rather conservative, I had one of the least desirable sales territories. I had to maintain a sense of humor to keep my sanity. One of my most challenging prospects was the manager in charge of office equipment at the Golden Grain Company. I'd been trying for months to get an appointment to sell him copiers or typewriters or a pencil sharpener, anything to make a sale, but to no avail. He was always busy, out of the office, or otherwise unavailable to me. I tried cold-calling him, but I couldn't get past his receptionist.

One day, as I was preparing to make yet another sales call at Golden Grain, I told my friend Ralph about the difficulty I was having. Ralph was a salesman too. He specialized in copiers. He was the guy you called in to make the really tough sales. I told him I could use some help with Golden Grain.

"Hey, remember the day we switched coats and had everybody in the office in stitches? Why don't we try that as an icebreaker with the receptionist?" he suggested.

Ralph and I were not exactly identical twins. Along with an obvious difference in skin tone, there was about a twelve-inch height differential. We were both wearing the standard IBM blue sport coats one day. He accidentally picked mine up off the back of a chair and put it on. The sleeves draped down past his knees. Just for laughs, I put his jacket on too. It fit like a glove. Literally, like a glove.

The people in our office had a good laugh, and Ralph thought it might loosen up the guardians of the gate at Golden Grain. I certainly did not have a better idea, so Ralph came along on my cold call. It turned out to be something of a wet call too. It was a hard rain even for Seattle, which is one of the soggiest cities in North America. To try to surprise the receptionist, Ralph and I swapped coats in the car. The mismatched twins walked into the office under a dripping umbrella. Ralph's arms were invisible. I looked like a badly dressed goalpost.

The receptionist didn't look up as we walked in—she was on the phone with someone. But she must have recognized my voice when I asked to see the vice president of operations. She looked up and seemed prepared to blow me off with another excuse.

When her eyes fell on Ralph and me, she exploded into laughter. I thought the woman was going to need oxygen.

After she finally caught her breath, she told the person on the phone that they'd better come see this. Then she changed her mind. "No, you guys walk on through the door and go through the main office all the way to the boss's office in the far corner. I want everyone to see this!"

For more than a year, I'd been the polite, well-mannered, nicely dressed IBM salesman who could not get past the receptionist at Golden Grain. As we went through the door into previously forbidden territory, I heard the secretary speed-dialing all of the Golden Grain managers, telling them to make sure and catch what was coming their way.

Ralph and I played it straight. We acted as though we could not imagine what they found so humorous. We didn't smile until we walked into the office of the vice president and he greeted us with a grin. "If you have the guts to walk in here dressed like that, the least I can do is listen to your pitch," he said.

Our act of humor enabled us to establish a key relationship with the company, which I believe IBM is still benefiting from today.

There are also health benefits to lightening up. When you're able to laugh at life, your body muscles expand and contract, your blood circulation increases, and your digestive system improves. The body produces endorphins, which facilitate the healing process. I recently read that fifteen minutes a day of deep gut laughter is equivalent to five minutes of moderate jogging. Learn to lighten up. It's an important step to staying motivated.

Attitude Tool 9
Exercising Will Help Keep You Motivated

Psychologist and researcher Diane Tice found that people use a wide variety of distractions to motivate themselves in trying to escape negative moods and the bad attitudes that accompany them. They read, watch TV, go to movies, or play video games to break their thought patterns. The problem is that unless you find a distraction that offers something uplifting, funny, or inspiring, your mood could get worse.

Tice found that one of the best ways to move to a more positive and motivated frame of mind was to exercise. A regular exercise routine can provide relatively quick positive feedback in the form of weight loss, muscle development, and a sense of doing something positive for yourself. Physical exertion moves us from a low-arousal state to a state of high arousal, according to Daniel Goleman, author of *Emotional Intelligence.*

Of course, it's not always possible to drop everything and run to the gym or track when you find yourself a little down, but there are some simple, quick exercises you can do while standing in line or sitting at your desk. I suggest taking a sixty-second mental vacation. Close your eyes, look up, put a big smile on your face, and begin to think about someone you love or something you love to do. Hold that thought, capture the moment, and begin to feel the peace, the joy, and the power of that experience.

Now you are equipped to seek your personal and professional success by using the tools in your Attitude Tool Kit and by practicing these daily guidelines.

Attitude Tune-Up

- Count your blessings daily, and give thanks.
- Get proper rest and exercise, and start eating more healthily.
- Do not let petty office or school politics have power over your personal or professional success. Monitor what you hear, what you read, and what you say.
- Set aside personal time with family and close friends.
- Help someone less fortunate. It brings out your true spirit.
- Feed your spirit daily; read and listen to motivational books and tapes.
- Discover the motives that motivate you, and remember, motivation is not permanent.
- Reflect on your victories—things you've forgotten that were special. Rekindle the fire that helps you turn your attitude into action.
- Create an upbeat, positive greeting that builds enthusiasm for you and everyone around you.
- Develop a clear vision, lock into your purpose and passion, and set goals with deadlines.

Don't forget, the best coach with the strongest power over your performance is the coach that lives within you.

CHAPTER EIGHT

Build Your A-Team

STEP 8
Build supportive relationships.

This step looks at how you can build the supportive relationships you need to achieve your personal and professional success. Having the right team, with the right attitude, makes it easy to turn your attitude into action.

Three years after venturing out on my own as a motivational speaker, I was invited to give my first speech before a group of two thousand peers at the annual National Speakers Association Conference. This is considered a rite of passage in my profession. I was excited! Unfortunately, instead of approaching the opportunity with an attitude of humility, I put a lot of pressure on myself to impress my colleagues. What they got that night was a lot of *Let me show you how good I am. Here's my best joke. Here's my best one-liner. Here's my signature story.*

I was certainly trying too hard to impress them. Later I came to realize that you really can't express when you're trying to impress. After finishing my twenty-minute "It's All About Me" talk, I received a standing ovation from my gracious and professional colleagues, which is customary at this event. Many offered congratulations and compliments, but as I listened to their praises I knew I had not hit the mark. I appreciated their kindness, but I realized that what I really needed at that moment was constructive feedback.

As those thoughts were running through my head, one of the top motivational speakers in the country walked up to congratulate me. As he approached, he nodded and said, "Good job." I replied, "Thanks, but what could I have done better?" He paused and stared at me for a moment or two. Then he reached into his pocket and pulled out what looked like a scorecard. "I've got some feedback. I can give you this, but when most people ask for constructive criticism, they can't handle it. Basically, I was scoring you for my own personal growth."

"I can handle it," I assured him.

He then shared his ratings of my speech. He'd given me scores for style, humor, enthusiasm, voice, and content. I scored high in several of those areas, but I missed the mark. The overall score he had on the card reflected my own appraisal, and what I felt in my spirit. Basically, I had delivered what I had prepared. I had practiced my presentation by focusing on my delivery and stories. I'd lost sight of how I could best serve my audience.

Even though I'd asked for his assessment, and I knew it was valuable and honest, it still hurt. The truth often does. But growth comes from our ability to embrace the truth even when it is painful. Later that evening, I shared my rating and the feedback I'd received from this trusted member of my team with a few other colleagues. They said they were disappointed in him. *How could he say that to you on one of your biggest nights as a professional speaker? You were great. You were wonderful. Everybody loved you.*

That night his constructive criticism served me better than their praise. Constructive feedback is invaluable, and having friends and co-workers who will give it to you is important and necessary for your growth. It may not be easy to take at the time it is given, but like me, you will learn to appreciate it over the long term.

We Are Formed by Many Hands and Hearts

After I'd given a speech to a business group, a well-dressed guy came up to me and introduced himself. He told me that he really enjoyed my presentation. He said he planned to use it in his business. I asked him what he did.

He puffed out his chest and said, "I'm a self-made man."

"You are?"

"Yep!" he said proudly.

I'm sorry, but no one makes it alone. Siegfried has Roy. Ben has Jerry, and Barnes had Noble. No man, or woman, is an island. We all need people in our lives. We need their perspectives, their wisdom, their honesty, and their support. The strength of our relationships is one of the greatest measures of the quality of our lives. To a large degree, the attitudes we have about ourselves and about the world are the result of the feedback we get day in and day out from the people around us. To build a winning attitude, you've got to have strong relationships with people who share your trust and interests. I call my supporters my Attitude Team, or simply my A-Team.

To build your A-Team, you sometimes have to let go of ego and adopt an attitude of humility, or one of service. You have to communicate honestly and tactfully. You have to trust others as well as yourself. Remember, if you're the student—and we all play the role of student from time to time—let the teacher teach. Even though you may not understand the lesson being taught at any given moment, eventually you will.

My A-Team consists of the people with whom I share the greatest trust and confidence. Our relationships have withstood the tests of time and temperament. My team is diverse. It's composed of women and men of all ethnic groups and social classes. Wise women have always been the core of my team, starting with my grandmother when I was a young boy, my mom, my aunts, and my sister. I've learned a lot from women. They seem to understand the complex nature of relationships and feelings. The members of my A-Team whom I've already mentioned include:

- My mom, who sent me to kindergarten feeling that I wasn't different because I stuttered, I was special. She taught me not to focus on the problem but on the solution and the necessary steps to meet the challenge or overcome the obstacle. She was the first person I knew who talked about keeping the "end result" in mind. She also taught me to use visualizations: "Now Keith, picture yourself standing up speaking clearly and people listening because you're speaking with confidence and enthusiasm. You're going to be standing up saying your name as loudly as you can and people will be clapping with approval." I always felt that my mother had confidence in my future success. It was as if she could see it coming, and she helped me see it too. She taught me to stay focused on the steps to make it happen. She taught me to practice with a purpose.

- My cousin Kenny Lombard, who gave up his Saturday mornings to help prepare me for a job with IBM. Kenny encouraged me to develop my skills. He became my career goal model. Kenny helped me understand my weaknesses and develop them into strengths. In the beginning, he believed in my potential more than I did.

- My co-worker Ralph Bianco had a very good business mind, and he shared his knowledge with me without ever asking for anything in return other than my friendship. He knew a lot about marketing, consulting services, and financial selling. Ralph was also a former Navy commander, so he understood leadership and teamwork. I worked closely with Ralph, and we developed a team that made the most of our individual skills. I was very good at doing my sales presentations and my product delivery demonstrations and would coach Ralph in those areas.

- One of my best friends, Calvin Saunders, trusted me by sharing something that was very personal to him. I'll tell you the story in just a few pages. It wasn't so much what he told me that mattered, it was the fact that he trusted me enough to share information that could bring criticism or mocking from others. We have been friends for thirty-one years, and it's all built on our mutual trust, shared vision, and core values.

- My dad. My father wasn't overly impressed with my athletic accomplishments because he was more concerned about my getting a good education. He'd always tell me, "You'd better get an education because even if you're blessed to play at the college level, you're going to have to have good grades. And even if you're abundantly blessed and able to play professional ball, you have to have something to fall back on. You can't play basketball all your life."

My father also stressed the importance of believing in myself. "Don't let anyone talk you out of your dream," he would say. He also had a knack for keeping me humble. After a good basketball game, I'd often come home to tell my dad how well I'd played. I think he worried about me getting overly confident. "Don't forget there's somebody else out there who is working harder, who's just as tall and probably better than you. Even though you're scoring a lot of points and you might be winning, you probably haven't met a worthy opponent, so you need to humble yourself and continue to work hard."

Today, I'm the creation and product of many loving, supportive, and dedicated people. I have a strong support team. I appreciate the value of having people who support me in my work and in my personal life.

Building Relationships with the Right Attitude

I attended a seminar conducted a few years ago by one of the leading self-help advocates in the world. This seminar on relationships was held in a vacation paradise resort. It cost more than $2,500 for the two-day session. Many of those who attended were successful executives, business owners, and entrepreneurs who had devoted their lives to their careers or their companies. In their drive for success, they had neglected their relationships. One after another, they offered their stories at this seminar. The themes were very similar. They'd reached the top. They'd made a lot of money and earned widespread recognition. But they had no one to share it with. Their relationships had been poorly constructed and neglected. As a result, they'd come to the seminar to learn how to rebuild them. Most of these people thought they had it all, until they realized that it meant nothing without someone to enjoy it with.

If you approach your relationships with an attitude of *What's in this for me?* or with an attitude of *I don't have time for anybody else*, one day you will probably find yourself alone and wondering where all of your friends have gone. The most powerful tool you have for building lasting and mutually beneficial relationships is a *service* attitude, in which your goal in every relationship is to add value to the other person's life.

Your goal should be to add to the quality of the lives of those people who have trusted you with their friendship. That means you are there for them when they need support and assistance. It means you aren't afraid to stand up for them when others are putting them down or when they've fallen out of favor. It means you focus on the best that is in them and try to help them express it even when they aren't focusing on the best in themselves. If you approach your relationships with that attitude, you will always be able to find shelter in the friendship and trust of others.

If you haven't put substantial effort into developing strong relationships, then you should not be surprised to find yourself dealing with attitudes of loneliness, rejection, and isolation.

Building Your Own A-Team

The people you allow to embrace your life ultimately have the greatest impact on your attitude.

I can't overemphasize the importance of building a solid A-Team. It's critical, especially during those times when you are looking for guidance and sharing confidences. Ultimately, when you engage in conversation with another person, you have no control over how they share the information. By building a team with shared visions and values, you reduce the chances of having confidences shared beyond the team.

I can count on my A-Team to help me keep my attitude positive. They also help me see with a wider range of vision. At every major turning point of my life, there has been someone there to help me find the learning point. I'm sure it's been the same way for you, even though in the day-to-day scramble, you may not have given much thought or enough credit to your own support team. It might be helpful for you to take some time to review your life and think of those who've made a difference.

Make a list of who's on your A-Team to remind yourself of all the people who have supported you and helped you when your circumstances or attitude took a turn for the worse. Then, the next time you're tempted to think you're all alone, rid yourself of that negative thought by visualizing all the people who support you and believe in you.

If you find yourself with a lackadaisical attitude, bogged down, unmotivated, and unwilling to get off your *If onlys*, *What ifs*, and *What nows*, I suggest you think again of all the effort other people have put into your life and try this affirmation: *I can't let down the people who believed in me and worked for me. It's time I started believing in and helping myself.*

When I'm alone and on the road, or whenever I'm feeling a little lonely or down, I get in touch with one or two, or depending on the depth of my mood, three or four of the people on my A-Team. I call them or e-mail them just to make contact. I try to catch up on their lives and see how they are doing. I find that's all I need, just to remind myself that I'm not alone. Of course, there are times when they call me. I want them to do that, because I want to contribute to their happiness and security too.

Relationships are built on two-way streets. They have to be mutually beneficial. Each side has to bring something of value. Otherwise they will not endure.

Networking Teams Are Built on Mutually Beneficial Relationships

Networking involves casting your net to connect with like-minded individuals and *working* toward establishing mutually beneficial relationships with them. Networking relationships are built upon an attitude of service and sharing.

Lynne Hellmer is a wonderful example of the power of a sharing attitude in networking relationships. Several years ago she decided to launch an "educational and inspirational initiative for working women as a one-time training activity." Lynne envisioned 125 women coming together to be inspired and motivated to grow and to learn. Clearly other women shared her vision and felt a need to participate, because over four hundred of them attended the first conference. Lynne Hellmer began with a modest dream that grew into a phenomenal event that now draws more than eight thousand women from around the country.

I met Lynne several years ago when she asked me to speak at the Biennial Conference for Working Women. Speaking before this audience of professional women was one of the greatest experiences in my life. I went to motivate and got motivated. I went to inspire them, and they, in turn, inspired me. I think women today are moving with an attitude of action.

From a workshop aimed at a few hundred university-based clerical workers, this award-winning biennial event now draws thousands of working women nationally to the University of Illinois campus every other spring. From the start, Lynne Hellmer's mission was important: to provide a forum in which working women at all levels can explore ideas and adopt innovative techniques that will help them rise to new levels of responsibility, recognition, and fulfillment. It is one of the nation's greatest networking events for women.

It offers programs and speakers whose primary purpose has been to educate, inspire, and motivate. While the theme of every conference is different, the underlying focus remains the same—to help women at all levels build confidence, create possibilities, and arrive at reasonable real-life solutions to the shared problems they face in their personal and professional lives.

It was evident when I first met Lynne that she had a can-do attitude. She has definitely put her attitude into action. She overcame the inevitable setbacks and hazards associated with coordinating a major conference and remained undaunted. She didn't envision it growing into such a phenomenal success and enriching so many, but when you do the right thing, and people with shared visions and values come together, your network grows.

While there is a tendency to overlook the fact that our needs are universal, Lynne was able to tap into other women's needs. Everyone benefits: the women who attend her conferences depart with more skills and tools to enhance their personal and professional lives, and Lynne embraces her passion and purpose. That mutual sharing represents the best of networking relationships.

Shared Values Are the Foundation

To build a team and create a network, your goal and desire should be to pursue what is important to you. In return, not only will you be rewarded, but your efforts could be far-reaching and beneficial for others. All effective teams should have shared visions and values and be working toward the same end result. It's very important to build your A-Team based on values.

Values are standards by which attitudes are formed. Values help you put your attitude into action. People move or gravitate toward what they care about or what they love.

> *Where your treasure is, your heart will also be.*
> —MATTHEW 6:21

Values help direct behavior and give us justification for our actions. My values for building my A-Team are the following:

- Integrity—living with high ethical standards
- Respect—treating all people with love and dignity
- Honesty—being truthful at all costs, being a doer of your word
- Accountability—recognizing the importance of personal responsibility
- Faith—having belief in your heart and hope and confidence in your spirit
- Love—having a foundation of support and unconditional love
- Health—being free of illness and physically fit
- Wisdom—having the ability to use your knowledge
- Compassion—having a loving spirit and a sincere desire to help others

- Achievement—accomplishing a feeling of success
- Recognition—being made to feel appreciated and important

My grandmother once told me that everything I accomplish will be the direct or indirect result of someone else's help. She taught me the importance of teamwork. There's really no limit to what can be accomplished when no one cares who gets the credit.

Evaluating Your Attitudes About Relationships

Let's look at the behaviors that are essential to building lasting and mutually supportive relationships.

1. *Accept others unconditionally.*
   Many people tend to have the attitude that their friends and family members should always live up to their expectations, be available to them at all times, always be in tune with their needs, agree with them, and see everything from their perspective. When you set those demanding requirements for your relationships, you're bound to be disappointed. Offer your friendship unconditionally, and you will be rewarded with theirs. Accept that your friends and loved ones will not always share your viewpoint or your agenda. They have their own perspectives, their own commitments to fulfill, and their own challenges with which to deal. If a person becomes involved in negative behaviors that are self-destructive or harmful to you or others, you should do what you can to help, but distance yourself if the relationship begins to have a negative impact on your own life.

2. *Earn trust by being trustworthy.*

   By offering unconditional kindness, honesty, and commitment to a relationship, you show yourself trustworthy and earn the trust of others. You can't expect people to honor you if you don't honor them. If you don't show up when you say you'll be there, if you don't help when you said you would, then you can't expect to be trusted the next time. You have to win trust one small step at a time and then keep earning it.

3. *Do nice things without expecting anything in return.*

   Offer a compliment. Write a note. Send a small gift. Random acts of kindness are wonderful gifts to others, but only if they come with no strings attached.

4. *Be loyal, even when it may not be the popular thing to do.*

   Loyalty involves honoring your friends when others belittle them. Guard the secrets they've entrusted to you. When I was in college, my friend Calvin was an All-Conference wide receiver on the football team. He was strong, lean, and mean. He was a great player and a proud leader of the team. One week during the school year, I noticed that Calvin was waiting at a bus stop every day after practice. I knew he had a car, so I couldn't figure out why he was taking the bus. My curiosity got the best of me, so I asked him where he was going on the bus. Initially he refused to tell me, but with continued prodding and under an oath of secrecy, he confided that he was taking ballet lessons. *Ballet lessons?*

   When he saw my reaction, he told me he'd read that his goal model, NFL All-Pro receiver Lynn Swann of the Pittsburgh Steelers, had taken ballet lessons to improve his balance and agility. If it was good enough for Lynn Swann, it was good enough for him. After he told me, Calvin seemed a little concerned that I might slip up and tell his secret, so I told him that to prove my trustworthiness I'd sign up for the class too! Calvin and I must have been quite a sight to our classmates. We actually had fun.

Loyalty also means helping and encouraging others to fulfill their promise. Sometimes this may mean telling them things they don't want to hear in order to motivate them to do more with their gifts. True friends don't always tell you what you want to hear; they tell you what you need to hear. Goethe said, "Treat people as they are and they remain that way. Treat them as though they were what they can be and we help them become what they are capable of becoming."

5. *Listen to others not to form judgments but to understand their point of view.*

In some ways, this is the easiest thing you can do for a person you care about. Listening is a simple thing, but doing it without judging can be difficult. You have to clear your mind and put your own experiences and values aside while you listen through the other person's heart and soul. You need to understand where they are coming from before you can offer your insight and advice. You want to make sure that the message being communicated is the message received, because ineffective communications can be costly.

Nine months after being launched, the $125 million Mars Climate Orbiter was destroyed as it began its initial orbit around the planet. More than 400 million miles from Earth, the NASA spacecraft became the victim of a communications snafu between two companies that routinely work together on space missions. One agency was transmitting crucial flight data in inches, feet, and pounds, while the other assumed that engineers had converted the data to metric units of millimeters and meters. Their lack of communication proved to be an expensive mistake and an embarrassment to the space program.

Remove Toxic Negativity from Your A-Team

I believe that when you live with the five attitudes described above, you will attract the sort of people who make for a supportive and reliable A-Team. It's vital that you surround yourself with caring, trustworthy, honest, positive, goal-oriented people. Their positive charge will motivate and inspire you. Their optimism will be contagious. Unfortunately, pessimism is also contagious, which is why you don't want to surround yourself with negatively charged people. Pessimists by nature present a danger to your attitudinal health. Here's a tip: If you ever need to borrow money, borrow from a pessimist, because they'll never expect to get it back.

Pessimism:
- Promotes depression
- Discourages action
- Causes anxiety and fear
- Is bad for your health
- Turns minor mistakes into setbacks, setbacks into disasters, and disasters into catastrophes

Sure, you have the ultimate control over how you choose to respond to negative influences, but why put yourself in a situation where you always have to be on the defensive? Negative people simply create an environment that makes it harder to stay positive. Their attitudes can corrupt yours and throw you off track.

Judges and Critics

These are people of narrow perspective who tend to devote considerable time and effort to judging and criticizing the actions of others. They are heavily into making moral and value judgments. Their approach ranges from being openly critical and demoralizing to offering such casual critiques as "I certainly wouldn't have done it that way."

Understandably, people with a judgmental attitude are repelled by an aura of optimism around anyone else. To them, optimism is the mark of someone who is naive, unrealistic, or shallow. The optimist's attitude is *Lead, follow, or get out of the way!* Some judgmental folks are filled with resentment. Others feel that they can't control their own lives so they attempt to control others. They expect everyone to live within their narrow view of what is right and wrong. We may not agree with them, but if we let them into our lives, they can infect our own attitudes and disrupt our plans.

Professional Victims

Do you know someone whom life happens to? I know that's an odd-sounding sentence, but these are odd people. They never make things happen. Things happen only *to* them. They say such things as "I should have gotten the job, but the boss has it in for me." Or "My project didn't work out because nobody else on my team wanted to do anything." Or "I can't get any of my assignments done because people keep calling me and wasting my time."

These people can be counted on only to botch things up and then blame someone else. They:

- Set their sights low
- Expect very little out of life

- Do nothing, so they won't risk failure
- Quit while they're ahead
- Settle for less than they want

Professional victims play the blame game. They take no responsibility. They'd like to help you out, but someone else is always getting in the way. They are helpless and hopeless and highly frustrating, so don't let them take up a spot on your A-Team. Post a sign: *No Victims Allowed!*

Soap Opera Stars

Do you ever watch the soaps? You can admit it, no one will jump out from behind the page and arrest you. For many people, soap operas are a guilty pleasure. They're certainly not boring. There are people, though, who think life is one big soap opera, minus the commercials. Like characters in a soap opera, these people often have over-the-top attitudes. They can be charming, charismatic, narcissistic, flamboyant, imaginative, compelling, and persuasive.

These soap opera pretenders love drama, and they love the limelight. They tend to see you as one of the supporting cast, or an extra put on the set merely to serve as a foil to their whims and fancies. They need an audience. You're it.

There are no intermissions, and the curtain never comes down. Their lives are a long-running series. Just when you think the end is near, they'll create another drama, dilemma, or crisis they cannot escape without you. They're control freaks, and you're the puppet they're stringing along. To validate their own lives, they need you around as a witness—not as a participant, or a lovable sidekick, just a witness. "I can't go on without you! You must save me!" is their cry. As soon as you try to get a speaking part, they step on your lines.

No matter how important the items on your agenda are or how badly you need to spend time doing something outside of their world, they won't see it. Their life is a stage. If you're smart, you'll head for the exit. Tell them you'll gladly read the reviews, but you don't have time for another opening, or another show.

Bitter to the Core

People with this attitude have a motto: *There's nothing worse than seeing your friends succeed.* These are unhappy people who gladly spread their misery around. They love company. They are angry, belittling, resentful, and at times vindictive. Sarcasm and biting humor are their favorite weapons, which they gleefully fire like poison darts. Their humor is hurtful and harmful. They have taken the bitterness pill as a cure for disappointment, hurt, or heartache, but it only makes their attitudes worse. Don't let them push their poison pills on you.

Creating a Nontoxic Zone

Though we may not be able to isolate or eradicate all toxic people, we may be able to limit our exposure to them and minimize their impact on our own attitudes. One way to do this is to give them wide berth to avoid contamination. Unfortunately, sometimes the toxic person is a relative or a loved one. If you can't avoid these people entirely, you should develop strategies for diluting or countering their influence. Here are proactive strategies for dealing with their lethal emissions.

Case Study: Disarming a Parent Who Has a Toxic Attitude

Noelle loves her father. Unfortunately, whenever she visits him, he makes judgments about her life and her friends and criticizes much of what she has done. She has adopted the attitude that she will not fall prey. Instead she seeks to rise above. She has learned to disarm and deflect his attitude rather than respond to it. When he makes quick judgments or criticizes her, she responds by finding something nice to say to him or by doing something kind. She shuts out the negative and focuses on the positive aspects of their relationship. It takes a great deal of self-control, but she has come to view it as a test of her strength and maturity. This strategy has worked well for Noelle. When her father becomes sarcastic, she offers him love and kindness. She models the behavior and attitude she wishes her father would offer to her. She has noticed him slowly beginning to respond.

Proactive Strategy: Rescuing the Wife/Victim

Charlie's wife tends to be a professional victim. She may not yet have passed her apprenticeship, but she's getting close. Whenever she falls into the victim mode, he walks her through all of the good things in her life to disarm her notion that "everything happens to me." He uses gentle humor as a weapon to defuse her sense of victimization by comparing her life to *I Love Lucy*. He then helps her develop strategies for being proactive and leads her into action, hoping that she will eventually get the sense that she can take responsibility for her own happiness and success.

The Best Defense Against Toxic People Attacks

It does no good to try and fight those in your life with negative attitudes. Your best hope is to stay centered and focused on maintaining your own positive and productive attitude.

It's not always easy, of course. But finding that proper balance will eventually come naturally to you so that whenever your positive attitude is threatened, you'll be able to center yourself mentally, focus on your long-term goals, and avoid being knocked off course. It is helpful, in difficult times, to call up the positive and supportive people who are on your A-Team. These are the people in your life who are consistently positive and upbeat. They take responsibility for their actions and are enthusiastic and encouraging of others. These are the people who take a proactive and responsive approach to life. These people believe in you and your ability to succeed.

Attitude Tune-Up

- Evaluate your attitude about relationships. Accept others unconditionally.
- Earn their trust by being trustworthy.
- Do nice things without expecting anything in return.
- Be loyal, especially when the person is not around.
- Listen to others, not to form judgments but to understand their point of view.
- Create a nontoxic zone to keep negative people from destroying your A-Team.

You are successful when you remember that somewhere, sometime, someone gave you a gift. That gift is what started you in the right direction. Remember that you are blessed when you pass that gift on to help someone else.

CHAPTER NINE

Develop a *Whatever-It-Takes* Attitude

STEP 9
See changes as an opportunity.

This step helps you embrace change. It is the key process for handling change as well as the strategies to accept it, leaving you with an attitude of willingness to take action.

After I made the difficult decision to leave IBM to become a professional speaker, I had one final hurdle to clear. I had to tell my father. As I noted earlier, Dad spent his entire thirty-six-year teaching career at the same community college. He believed in job security, loyalty, and sticking with a job through thick and thin. He is not a guy who readily embraces or regularly seeks change in his life.

He knew I had mortgage and car payments that were considerable even for a single guy. He also knew that I had no speaking engagements lined up. No long-term clients. No guarantees. So I was not surprised that after I broke the news of my career change, he had a few questions and concerns.

"Son, it's not going to be easy. Do you have a contingency plan if this speaking thing doesn't work out? You've got a mortgage and car payments, and you don't have any clients. Let me ask you a few questions. Are you prepared to get a roommate?"

"Whatever it takes, Dad."

"Rent out the house and move into an apartment?"

"Whatever it takes, Dad."

"Get a second job?"

"Whatever it takes."

"Sell your car?"

"Whatever it takes."

"Move home with your mother?"

"Dad, if I have to move back home, live in the basement, and sleep in the bunk bed, that's what I'll do. I am going to make it on my own because I know what I'm doing right now is what I'm supposed to do."

I had towered over my father physically since the age of twelve, but I think this was the first time I'd ever stood up under his interrogation. He fell silent for a minute or two, appraising me, weighing my resolve. I was a student receiving one final evaluation.

"Keith, you've convinced me. Son, you've got WIT."

"What are you talking about, Dad?"

"You've got a *Whatever-It-Takes* attitude—WIT. And that's what it's going to take for you to make it out there on your own."

With my dad's blessing, and a *Whatever-It-Takes* attitude, I launched a career that has been financially rewarding and spiritually fulfilling. The risks were well worth the rewards, believe me. Any time you want to stretch and grow, you are going to have to make changes and take risks. Change is part of life, and risk is part of the change process. To deal with risk and change, you have to adopt a *Whatever-It-Takes* attitude.

We make changes and take risks all our lives—driving on the freeway, starting a relationship, investing in the stock market, switching careers, moving to new jobs—it's part of living. If you're not making changes and taking risks in some aspect of your life, you are probably in a rut. Your attitude toward all aspects of your life probably reflects that rut. Bad attitudes can arise when we feel we aren't moving forward with our lives, often because we are resisting making a change or taking a necessary risk.

Change Your Attitude, Change Your Altitude

As someone who reached adult height while still in grade school, I went through serious growing pains. My shins and knees seemed to ache at night. It hurt, and it was a little scary. My mom told me it had something to do with "growth plates." She explained that I should accept the aches and pains gladly because they meant my body was changing, that I was growing fast.

I thought of her explanation during my transition from IBM employee to free agent on the professional speaking circuit. Aches and pains, confusion, and misgivings often accompany change. When you're pursuing your dreams, it's inevitable that you will experience doubts and fears.

At some point, each of us will be faced with a major life change, an incident that alters our life in such a way that we are never quite the same. Major life changes include moving, marriage, death, surgery, divorce, promotion, demotion, retirement, ending a relationship, pregnancy, change in income level, and birth. It's possible for a major life change to have both positive and negative effects. When you face a major change, you can expect that you will go through a great deal of turmoil and anxiety as you question yourself. It helps to know that it's all part of the process of growing. It may hurt a little now, but in the long run you will see the benefits of embracing change in your life.

The other day I was on a flight, and the pilot announced that we should fasten our seat belts because there was some turbulence ahead. What did I do? I looked out the window for the turbulence. Didn't see a thing. Didn't buckle my seat belt. If you happen to be on a Delta 767 and notice a huge dent in the bottom of the overhead compartment, you'll see evidence of what happens when a six-foot–six-inch man doesn't pay attention to the pilot's warning about turbulence.

My best advice is always to be on the alert for change. After all, change is one of the few constants we have in this world. If you don't believe me, take a look at your day planner or wall calendar. How many cross-outs and time and place changes can you identify? Many, if you're like most people. A meeting is changed from Monday morning to Tuesday afternoon. A project is due on Thursday instead of Friday. A test has been moved to next week. It's up to you to stay flexible—to "go with the flow." If you try to fight it, your attitude will suffer, and so will your performance. If you stay flexible, you'll continue to be constructive.

Adopt the attitude that change is to be expected, and you'll be a lot better at dealing with it. You'll be ready to embrace the change by learning that new technology, moving to that new position, or relocating to that new home.

A friend of mine recently became an "empty nester" when the last of her children moved out. This can be a difficult change for parents, but she took a positive attitude, embraced the change, and welcomed the opportunities that presented themselves. She was finally in a position to accept more responsibility at work. She'd held back from taking a promotion for five years because of family obligations, but when her children moved away from home, her work life filled up. "For the first time in twenty years, I was only accountable to me, no other human being," she told me. "No one was home wondering when I would get there. I didn't need to wonder if the children had had their dinner or if they'd been picked up from practice or if they were doing their homework. No, for the first time I was concentrating on *my* work and *my* needs. What an awesome revelation."

Many parents, particularly mothers, in her situation experience loneliness and isolation, but my friend chose to embrace the change in her life. The difference? Her attitude! Instead of viewing the departure of her children as a loss, she chose to see it as an opportunity. "Certainly there was a new void in my house, but that didn't need to translate to a void in my life," she said. "I still had the same wonderful friends and supportive family. And now I had time. Don't get me wrong. There are times when I feel lonely. I miss the children and family life. And that's OK. I just reflect on the positive memories, smile, and move on. Just because the nest is empty doesn't mean your life has to be!"

Another change many people have difficulty dealing with is one that happens gradually but seems to occur overnight—aging. The years slip by, and we are suddenly much older than we feel. Some people accept this change gracefully; others become bitter, fearful, or withdrawn.

I recently had the pleasure of meeting a seventy-year-old woman possessed of beauty, great presence, and style. She inspired me because of her attitude about embracing change and her willingness to take risks at this stage of her life. When I asked her what she did for a living, she said, "I'm a student. I'm working on my Ph.D. at Pacific Grove Graduate Institute." Leah Friedman told me that her life really changed at fifty when she became an empty nester. After her daughters graduated from college and left home, she embarked on a personal journey that included working as a fine art photographer, learning French, horseback riding, and returning to college.

"I like being old," she told me. "It's the best time of my life. I don't want to avoid the term, and I don't want people to avoid it with me. It's OK, it's good; there's nothing wrong with being old and calling it old. The important thing about being seventy is that I define what seventy is by who I am and the way I live. I don't have to conform to what somebody else thinks seventy is or what society says seventy is. We define the age; the age does not define us."

Now there's an attitude worth emulating. Leah Friedman has found that the key to eternal youth lies in a positive attitude. She refuses to give in to stereotypes. She has not let changes in her age define her. She defines herself through her wonderful attitude.

Change and Risk Management

Because of the turbulent nature of the workplace today, I'm frequently asked to speak to employees and managers about managing change and risk. The pace in downsizing, restructuring, and reengineering has slowed compared with a few years ago, but mergers, acquisitions, and reorganizations are in the headlines every day: MCI WorldCom bids $115 million for Sprint; Time Warner and Turner Broadcasting team up; Viacom agrees to buy CBS; Sumitomo and Sakura merge; Netscape becomes a unit of America Online; ABC and Disney form a global company; Qwest Communications International and US West approve a merger agreement.

With each shift in the corporate culture, employees face changes that affect them personally and professionally. Often they have to make decisions that involve risk. More and more people are making decisions similar to mine—opting to pursue their passions by working as free agents, independent consultants, or entrepreneurs with their own businesses. Others are regularly asked to change departments, work on special projects, or move to new divisions, and they too have choices to make, risks to take, and challenges to face.

It helps to understand what you are going through when faced with change. Otherwise you may find yourself swept up emotionally and mentally and wondering what hit you. There are two types of change: *planned* and *unplanned*. Planned changes are those that you choose in order to improve your life in some way. You take additional courses. You learn a new skill. You begin a fitness program. Since you make it happen, there is still a sense that you have control of your life. Unplanned changes are those that are forced upon you by circumstances beyond your control. A flat tire. Being downsized. A health problem. The death of a friend or family member. These are all stressful changes that can throw you off balance. But you can control the attitude that you choose to take toward the changes.

Those who resist change suffer from what I call *changecosis*, a disease that threatens your ability to enjoy life and to develop your full potential. When confronted by change, do you generally become rigid? Do you overreact? Become suspicious? Begin to blame others? Deny that it bothers you? Do you experience the *Yes, but* . . . syndrome? If you answered yes to any of these questions, there is a good chance you have changecosis.

My sister, Toni, told me about Bill a co-worker who apparently had a very serious case of this career-threatening ailment. Toni was one of the first women to become a commander with a big city police department. As you might imagine, she did not rise to that position by being a meek or shy woman. She is tough—in her own feminine way, of course. When she was promoted to commander, she made several changes within the department. Some new managers might be tempted to settle in for six months or so before making big changes. Toni prefers to "create chaos and then give everyone six months to get used to it."

Policemen are not likely to suffer in silence. Three or four officers were not happy, but Bill was having a particularly difficult time with the new commander and her changes. He made the mistake of sending a message out to his fellow officers on their mobile computers, saying that he might be going "postal" because his assignment had been changed. He thought he was making a joke, but my sister didn't think it was funny for a man who carries a gun to be making light of his mental state. She ordered him to take a psychological evaluation to determine if he really was having a difficult time adapting to change. He agreed to go into counseling and has improved his attitude, she said.

Many people have a great fear of change. Sometimes they even prefer to remain in an unpleasant or negative situation rather than leave what is known for something less familiar. This can be the dynamic in abusive relationships, when the abused person clings to the familiar, as bad as it may be.

A friend, who finally learned to accept a change that has greatly affected her life for the better, told the following story to me:

> I didn't plan it this way. I never thought that my marriage would end. We had been married for ten years. I'd known my husband since I was twelve years old. Yet there I was sitting in my counselor's office trying to determine what I had done wrong. In reality, I had done nothing wrong. The marriage was no longer healthy. I was married to an alcoholic. He had made the marriage almost impossible. But something was holding me back. Something was keeping me in this very unhealthy, unsafe relationship. Through counseling I found out it was fear.
>
> I had always been self-sufficient. I was well educated and had a good career. I was quite capable of surviving or even thriving on my own. I still owned a home that I had prior to the marriage. I had a little money saved. My car was paid for. Yet I found it difficult to leave. Certainly I still loved my husband, but that wasn't why I had not left already. That didn't happen until I recognized that my need to leave outweighed my love for him. My counselor and I set target dates, circled them on the calendar, and made a checklist of things that needed to be accomplished. Those dates came and went along with the excuses. The bottom line was, I was afraid to make the change.
>
> It took six more months of counseling before I overcame my fear of the unknown and made the move. I had been afraid of failing as a wife, fearful of living single in what I thought was a "married" world. I was afraid of starting all over again. Until I changed my attitude, I could not change my life. Until I could see the positive

of healthy living, I was doomed to my unhealthy status. I made the change. The results were immediate and fulfilling. I created an environment that was healthy for me. Today I live a very healthy, thriving life. I am mentally and emotionally strong, my career is great, and I have developed great friendships, including one with my ex-husband. Change can be for the better. Sometimes we just have to overcome our fear of it.

How Do You Respond to Change?

The type of attitude you adopt toward change determines whether you let circumstances and events control your life or whether you take control.

There are four basic ways to respond to change:

1. *Shift into neutral.*
   When the first downsizing was announced at IBM, some of my co-workers automatically made the assumption that their lives would not be touched. In essence, they went into serious denial. They decided to ignore this massive change in IBM's basic philosophy. Believe me, they did not remain neutral or unaffected for long. Sooner or later, their jobs and their lives were altered because of this change.
2. *Adopt a negative attitude.*
   Among my co-workers, the overwhelming response was negative—the typical knee-jerk response to change, and highly understandable. The negative reactions ranged from sarcasm to intense anger on the part of those who felt the most threatened and betrayed. Many complained excessively.

3. *Adopt a counterproductive attitude.*

Employees in one department were told that 30 percent of them would be laid off within six months. The attitude among those workers became subversive and counterproductive. They decided that since the company was letting them go and violating their trust, they were not going to do their jobs. They undermined the change and may well have hurt their ability to get referrals for jobs outside IBM.

4. *Adopt a positive attitude.*

Obviously this is the response that I believe benefits you the most. It may not be your initial reaction. Yet after you've had some time to reflect, it is generally possible to find a positive way to respond to change. Those at IBM who were confident of their skills seemed to take the most positive attitude. They believed in their value in the marketplace, and some looked forward to the challenge of finding a new job, maybe one that offered even greater security or a better place to raise their families. They exercised their power of choice and responded in an affirming manner. They had their concerns, sure, but they accepted the challenge of change and set about meeting it.

Understanding the Process of Change

To overcome fear of change, you first need to recognize the natural stages of the change process and understand that we all go through emotional and mental stress at some level when faced with change. You are not alone in feeling anxiety or dread. It is a part of life.

Stage One: Have I Got What It Takes?

This is the stage in which your fears of taking risks run the strongest. It's the terrifying point when you are standing on the high dive questioning whether you should make the leap. Are you more afraid of the humiliation of climbing down the ladder and going back to the way things were, or of jumping off, hitting the water, and making a splash?

This is often the most tortuous period of the change process, because you actually have the opportunity to go back to the comfort zone, or at least back to the known versus the unknown. But you can't move ahead by holding on. You have to let go. Understand that it is natural to feel some fear, some sense of loss, some trepidation, but you are also going to experience the exhilaration of a new experience, the rush of making a leap and pursuing new options and new opportunities. Accept both sets of feelings as natural to the process, and then decide that you are going to do whatever it takes to move ahead.

Stage Two: How Much Is This Going to Hurt?

Once you've let go and made the leap, you will experience the disorientation and insecurity of free-falling. You'll feel ungrounded, a bit lost, and maybe even a little nostalgic for the way things used to be. You may feel as if you've just made a huge mistake. Hang on.

I was afraid at first, but I realized that what is inside of me is greater than what is going on around me. You have to have faith. Fortunately for me, I have a strong belief in the power of prayer, trust in the Lord, and have a lot of people praying for me.

Understand that negative emotions and fears are going to crop up, but focus on where you are going, not where you've been. You've made it this far. Keep moving ahead, doing whatever it takes. Create positive affirmations. Listen to motivational tapes. Surround yourself with positive, dynamic people who are moving forward with their lives too.

Stage Three: Action Produces Results

By observing toddlers learning to walk, you can see how their confidence grows with each step. With each bit of forward progress, they are rewarded for taking a risk and managing their response to change. Of course, there are perils ahead. Overconfidence and inexperience will probably mean a few bumps on the head and skinned knees. You may feel joyous one minute and anxious the next; confident and then self-conscious. It's all part of the process.

When you embrace change as a natural part of life, you'll learn to welcome new opportunities and new challenges too. Your fears will diminish and your confidence will grow as you assert more and more control over your life. There may be some setbacks, but having taken risks and survived, you will feel a new self-assurance.

A period of change calls for taking action, planning, and reflection. It's wise here to take things one at a time and not allow yourself to become overwhelmed. Maintaining a balance between work and relationships is very helpful. It's also a time to call upon your faith and spirituality.

Stage Four: Whatever It Takes!

Welcome to the new you! You still need to understand that there are going to be challenges in your life. Maintain confidence in your ability to handle change.

At this point you want to avoid settling into another comfort zone. Instead, make a conscious effort to look ahead and to stretch yourself by setting new goals that include your work and relationships but also extend to making a difference in the larger arena of your community.

Ten Strategies for Creating Positive Attitudes About Change

1. Tap Into the Power of Your Subconscious

Take the opportunity to program your mind with a positive attitude about the ongoing change. Instead of hitting the snooze button and whining about the challenges presented by changes in your life, get up out of bed and thank your Creator for giving you another day to savor life. Then spend several minutes creating a plan for the day and a strategy for dealing positively with the challenges ahead.

I developed a habit of waking up and clapping my hands a few times to welcome the new day and get myself psyched up for the challenges it presents. Sometimes I feel a little weird, but I do it anyway because, if nothing else, it makes me laugh at myself, and laughter is always a good way to start the day.

2. Pause to Reflect

The late coach of the Green Bay Packers, Vince Lombardi, was one of the greatest motivators in professional football. He had his players look in a mirror before every practice and game, telling each of them to ask himself, *Am I looking at the person who is helping me win or one who is holding me back?* When you look in the mirror, you see the person who can do the most to improve your life, change your attitude, elevate your standards, and overcome your limitations.

While you are looking in the mirror, monitor your inner dialogues too, and be alert to any negative inner thoughts or self-criticisms regarding the change you are dealing with. Visualize yourself clearing out the negativism and pessimism and replacing it with an optimistic attitude.

3. Keep Your Long-Term Goals in Mind

Well-defined goals keep you focused on the end result. Visualization helps a great deal in these situations. I believe that if you can see it in your mind, you can make it happen.

When you focus on your goals, you regain a sense of control over your life, your self-esteem increases, and you sense that what happens around you doesn't have to affect what is within you.

4. Avoid Learned Helplessness

It's been estimated that 90 percent of the VCRs in this country have not had their blinking clocks set, because their owners feel it's too complicated to program them. Most people never even try. That is learned helplessness. Many of my co-workers at IBM became highly skilled at this. *I can't do anything about what's happening to me with this change, so why should I try?* Why? Because if you don't act on life, it will act on you. If you don't find direction for your life, it will direct you. If you don't decide where you are going, life will take you to a place you probably never wanted to be.

You may not be able to stop an unwanted change from occurring in your life, but you can program yourself to take positive actions that make the most of it. You are not helpless. You have enormous power to act, to set goals, and to go after them. There are millions of people in this world who have overcome tremendous challenges and succeeded.

5. Maintain a Balance

Handling an unplanned or even an expected change can be challenging. That's why it's important to maintain physical, mental, and spiritual balance. Rest, healthy eating habits, and regular exercise are important. Quality time with family and friends away from the pressures of work can provide a necessary social outlet.

Sometimes we fail to grasp the impact of a change on the various aspects of our life. Be conscious of how it affects your attitude toward work, family and loved ones, your financial security, and your faith, and work at remaining positive in your dealings in other aspects of your life.

6. Acknowledge Change

You should not ignore change. Sometimes the best way to make a major leap in life is to let go and strive for something better. Letting go empowers you to release past hurts, rejection, and frustration. Accepting change can take time. Generally it's a gradual process. Ultimately the only thing you can change is yourself, and sometimes that changes everything.

7. Convert Threats into Opportunities

When a change seems threatening, you can reframe it as an opportunity. A friend of mine worked in a department that underwent a complete overhaul. People who'd held comfortable jobs for years were given new assignments. Many of them fought it. Some quit. There was a great deal of bitterness. My friend wasn't happy about it either. He'd had a great job, but he'd always known that the day would come when he'd be asked to do something else. It was the nature of his business. He accepted a transfer to a more demanding, less enjoyable job, but he chose to see it as an opportunity to widen his experience and expand his knowledge. Not surprisingly, he thrived, while many of his former co-workers remained embittered and unhappy.

8. Turn the Change into a Challenge

Martin Luther King, Jr. said, "The ultimate measure of a man is not where he stands in moments of comfort, but where he stands at times of challenge and controversy." Challenges teach you something about yourself. So does change. Challenges force you out of your comfort zone. So does change. Challenges help you realize again what is most important to you. Change can do the same.

9. Turn on the Positive Energy

When I feel a potentially negative change coming on, I react the same way I do when I'm developing a cold: I do everything I can to build up my natural resistance. With the cold, I take vitamins and food supplements, and I increase my daily workouts to build up strength. In the case of a negative change, I create affirmations that I repeat in the mornings, afternoons, and evenings. I also tap into my list of quotations on the positive power of change.

> *Why settle for so little in life when you can have so much, just by daring to be different in your thinking.*
>
> —CATHERINE PONDER

> *You have stripped off the old self with its practices and have clothed yourselves with the new self, which is be[*renewed in knowledge according to the image of its cr[*
>
> —COLOSSIAN[*

What lies behind us and what lies before us are tiny matters compared to what lies within us.

—OLIVER WENDELL HOLMES

WORDS TO CHANGE BY

When change comes into your life, it is helpful to develop your own positive affirmations that will help you keep a positive attitude. I've come up with a few examples to help you create your own.

- I accept the reality of this change, and I intend to convert this "threat" into an opportunity for even greater accomplishment.
- I acknowledge that change is an essential part of life, and I am focused on finding solutions, not dwelling on problems caused by this change.
- I will take this change one step at a time to keep it manageable. I'll focus first on the easiest challenges to build my confidence and a pattern of successful change management.
- I will not put off meeting the challenges of this change. I will begin today to build a better tomorrow through change. I understand that I cannot fix what I will not face.
- I will do whatever it takes to master this change and to create balance in my life.
- For every door that has closed, I will find two that have opened because of this change.
- I will make the changes within myself that are necessary to handle the changes going on around me.
- I will look to my family, friends, trusted role models, and advisers to help me through this change.

- I will be patient and let the four stages of change unfold without panicking or trying to push the process along.
- I will celebrate each small step through this change process, and I will practice gratitude for the blessings I've received.

It can also be helpful to look back at changes that you've gone through in the past and focus on the positive outcomes and the positive attitude you developed once you'd gone through the change.

10. Seek Support from Members of Your A-Team

That's why you work on building and nurturing relationships, so that you'll be able to draw upon them in times of need. The people who truly care about you want you to lean on them in difficult and challenging times because then they know you will be there for them. My grandmother has always been there for me, so I have tried to do the same for her. Our roles have been reversed in the last few years as she has become more dependent and I've become more self-reliant, but our relationship is still strong.

Adapting to Change

Paralyzed from the neck down by a spinal cord injury sustained in an automobile accident, Barbara spent five months in the hospital. She says she didn't have time to get depressed because it took all her energy to recuperate. She maintained a positive attitude during this traumatic period of change in her life by taking joy in the small steps toward recovery. Unable to raise her hand for months to feed herself, she took pleasure in her ability to brush her teeth. The first time she pushed her wheelchair ten feet across a tile floor by herself, she cried. Each accomplishment was celebrated.

One of her goals was to walk out of the building when she was discharged from the hospital. She didn't make it far, but she did it. When she got home, there was a whole new set of challenges. Still she remained positive and active. She needed mental stimulation and decided to return to work. There she manages with a walker, but at home she continues to use her wheelchair because it's easier, particularly doing housework. She has also learned to ask for help, though that was not part of her nature either. "Sometimes you just don't have a choice," she said. "Things aren't easy, but they're not all that bad. I just do the best I can. My priorities have changed, and some things just aren't that important anymore. I try to enjoy myself as much as possible and live each day as if it were my last. It very nearly was! My story is not finished yet. It's a work in progress. My ultimate goal is to walk without a walker, and who's to say I won't."

Risky Business

With every change comes risk. But we lessen the risk of negative consequences when we take a positive attitude as Barbara has done. Risk is unavoidable, but we have a choice about how we view changes in our lives. Whenever I get on a plane, I'm taking a risk. I have to trust the pilot's ability, the safety of the plane, and have faith that God is overseeing the journey. Every time I stand in front of an audience, I'm taking a risk—a risk of possible rejection, a risk that I might forget part of my speech. By taking the attitude that I'll do whatever it takes to stay focused, make an impact, and deliver a positive message, I've found that I'm willing and able to accept the risk.

After all, history is on the side of many risk-takers who have reaped rewards in this world. Consider just a few:

- When Wilma Mankiller decided she wanted to become the first woman to serve as principal chief of the Cherokee Nation of Oklahoma, she knew there were many risks involved. In case she didn't understand the risks, there were reminders in the form of vandalism and death threats during her campaign. In winning the historic tribal elections of 1987, she revitalized her tribe, rebuilt its sense of community, and won the nation's admiration as a woman of courage and great spiritual strength.

- Steve Jobs and Steve Wozniak tried to get venture capitalists in Silicon Valley to invest in their idea for a computer, but they were told their idea would never fly. They took the risks anyway and led the entrepreneurial tidal wave in high-tech.

- Charles Darrow sent his game idea to Parker-Brothers, but they politely declined the idea. They cited fifty-two reasons why the game would never sell, including the fact that nobody was interested in making a game of real estate holdings. Fortunately for Parker-Brothers, Darrow was persistent. His game, Monopoly, became the best-selling game of all time.

- Bill Lear created the first car radio. People told him that it would never work because it would be too distracting to drivers. Unfortunately for him, he believed them and sold his idea to Galvin Manufacturing Company, later renamed Motorola. Then Lear came up with a plan for a company that built personal and corporate aircraft. This time he ignored all the naysayers, and Lear Jets became an industry leader.

- When Fred Smith wrote a paper for a business management class that proposed creating an overnight delivery service that competed with the U.S. Postal Service, his professor at Yale told him that though the concept was interesting and well formed, it wasn't feasible. He got a C. A little later, his company, Federal Express, was earning straight A's and millions and millions of dollars.

When you're open to losing something in order to gain something else, you're ready to take a risk. Taking risks requires stepping outside your comfort zone while standing on faith. Your willingness to take the risk may well determine how rewarding and fulfilling your life turns out to be. If you've been discouraged from taking a risk by what someone said to you, or by your own fears, you are not alone. We all hear discouraging words when we make a move to create a change in our lives. If you believe in your dreams, sometimes you have to go against popular wisdom. Take heart from the fact that most major accomplishments are made in spite of those fears and doubts. Consider these discouraging words that went unheeded, with lasting results:

- "This 'telephone' has too many shortcomings to be seriously considered as a means of communication."

  —WESTERN UNION, 1876

- "Heavier-than-air flying machines are impossible."

  —LORD KELVIN, PRESIDENT, ROYAL SOCIETY, 1895

- "Everything that can be invented has been invented."

  —COMMISSIONER, U.S. OFFICE OF PATENTS, 1899

- "Stocks have reached what looks like a permanent plateau."
  —IRVING FISHER, YALE PROFESSOR
  OF ECONOMICS, 1929

- "I think there is a world market for maybe five computers."
  —THOMAS WATSON, CHAIRMAN, IBM, 1943

- "We don't like their sound, and guitar music is on the way out."
  —DECCA RECORDING CO.,
  REJECTING THE BEATLES, 1962

- "But . . . what is it good for?"
  —IBM ENGINEER COMMENTING ON THE
  MICROCHIP, 1968

- "640K ought to be enough for anybody."
  —BILL GATES, 1981

- "A cookie store is a bad idea. Besides, the market research reports say America likes crispy cookies, not soft and chewy cookies like you make."
  —A POTENTIAL INVESTOR'S RESPONSE TO DEBBI
  FIELD'S BUSINESS PROPOSAL, AUGUST 1977

Positive change often comes in giant leaps. You may have to leave many doubts and doubters behind when you take risks, but the rewards are very often the greatest of your lifetime. Accept change as part of your life, make wise decisions, and take risks when they offer to improve the quality of your life.

Attitude Tune-Up

- Embrace change with a *Whatever-It-Takes* attitude.
- Count opportunities versus losses.
- Celebrate yourself: who you are presently and who you would like to become.
- Take your time. Change doesn't happen overnight.
- Be quick to listen and slow to speak.
- Change your attitude and change your life.
- Eliminate changecosis.
- Understanding the process of change starts by asking yourself these questions:

  Do I have what it takes?

  How much is it going to hurt?

  Will my actions produce the results I need?

The choice is yours. Change is the essence of life. Embrace it.

CHAPTER TEN

Make a Mark That Cannot Be Erased

STEP 10
Leave a lasting legacy.

In this final step, you'll uncover the power of turning attitude into action by discovering the importance and self-fulfilling reward of making a difference in the life of someone else.

Before I started my own business, I read a book entitled *Releasing Your Potential* by Dr. Myles Munroe. Two weeks later, by coincidence (or divine intervention), we met on an airplane. He told me about a sixteen-year-old young man who lived in Ghana. He came from a very poor village. All he ever wanted to do in his whole life was to make a difference in the lives of others. As a teen, he left home in search of riches and wealth to bring back to his village. He eventually ended up working on a cocoa plantation.

For seven years, he had no contact with his friends or his family. One day he returned to the village. The people gathered around, and someone asked, "What do you have to show for seven years of being away? What did you bring us? Where are the riches?"

The young man responded by reaching into his pocket and pulling out three tiny seeds.

"Is this all you have to show? Three tiny seeds?" someone asked.

Without speaking a word, he turned, went to the family hut, and planted those three seeds nearby. From those seeds grew the first cocoa plant to be cultivated in his nation. And the second and third as well. Today, cocoa is one of the primary crops in Ghana. According to legend, it was started by one African man who planted three tiny seeds.

Dr. Munroe told me that story and said, "Go plant some seeds. Go do some positive things for others. God's going to bless you. Remember, there are some people who will say they're going to help you in life, but they really won't. Don't depend on them because in many cases they won't have the information, the wisdom, or the insight to help you get where you need to go. Why? Because they are seedless. There are other people who will bless you, for they will give you the seeds of life. These are the people who will connect to your dream and your passion and help you move forward.

"When you go to the supermarket, sometimes you'll see two kinds of fruit, seedless fruit and fruit with seeds, but you don't know the difference until you look inside. And that's the way it is with certain people. You don't really know who they are until you look within them.

"I want you to plant yourself like a seed because, like a seed, the outer shell is going to die off, and when that happens you will cast off all of your past negative experiences.

You're going to become grounded in what your purpose is and what you're supposed to do. And you're going to endure some long winter nights and some hot summer days. There's a price you'll pay for living your dream. You'll have to make some sacrifices, but it will be worth it if you're willing to stay committed. You're going to take root. When you're rooted, you'll become fully committed, and you'll be unswayable. No one will be able to talk you out of achieving your purpose. One day, you're going to come up through the soil, you'll start to rise, to take action, and the momentum will carry you forward. When you surface, you'll see the results of your efforts, and you'll know that you're ready to make a difference. You'll be ready to plant some positive things—seeds—in other people."

I understood exactly what Dr. Munroe meant. After our plane landed in Atlanta, we learned that there was a delay for his connecting flight. "I'm supposed to spend two more hours with you," he said. We talked about life for a while longer. He told me about his upcoming leadership conference in the Bahamas. He invited me to come. I opened up my day planner to check the date. IBM had me booked up all week except for Friday. That was the day he was scheduled to speak.

As it turned out, I got there in time to hear him speak for two hours, and it was well worth the trip. In two hours I got what some people will never get in a lifetime. I learned that the most important thing we can do with our lives is to understand our purpose and release our potential so that we can plant positive seeds—seeds of hope, love, encouragement, and faith—in the lives of others.

I'm thankful today for all the positive things that God, my pastor, my family, and my friends have planted in me. In the previous chapters, I've shared with you my philosophy,

methods for assessing, managing, and monitoring your attitude, and practical ways of applying those methods to your
everyday life. I've introduced you to a process that allows
you to transform your positive attitude into positive action.
My goal has been to help you recognize that your attitude
makes a difference in everything you do. No matter what has
happened to you in the past, no matter what state you are in
at any given moment, you have the power to turn your life
around and to pursue your goals and dreams by adopting an
empowering attitude and taking the actions necessary to
move forward.

Sharing Wisdom Earned the Hard Way

I've had my challenges, but they certainly pale in comparison
with those faced by many others. My friend Art Berg is one
of the most inspirational people I know. He was twenty-one
years old, had just started his own tennis court construction
company, and was about to marry his fiancée when a friend
went to sleep at the wheel with Art in the car. It crashed into
an embankment, and Art was thrown from the vehicle. His
neck was broken, leaving him with little use of either his
arms or his legs. His doctors said he'd probably never be able
to work, never have children, and never compete in sports.

He lost his business, and for a long time he was unable
to get a job. He was advised to forget trying to lead a normal
life and to accept his "handicap." But Art had not lost his
positive attitude about life. One of his favorite affirmations is
by Napoleon Hill: "Nothing bad ever happens without equal
or greater benefit in return."

Art chose to believe that, and he chose this attitude: "I
decided that this could be the greatest experience of my life."

Determined to be self-reliant, he convinced Bell Atlantic to hire him by telling the company that if he didn't outsell their top producer in thirty days, he would leave without cashing a paycheck. He won three national awards for sales excellence in his first three years there. He married his fiancée, and they moved to Utah, where he opened a chain of bookstores. In 1992 he was named regional Young Entrepreneur of the Year. He then wrote a book, *Some Miracles Take Time,* and started Invictus Communications Inc., in Provo, Utah, to manage his public speaking career. Today he is one of the top professional speakers in the country.

Such a devastating blow might have embittered him, but instead Art is one of the most optimistic, enthusiastic, and giving people I know. In addition to everything else he has accomplished without benefit of his arms or legs, Art has become a world-class wheelchair athlete. On July 10, 1993, he set a world record by becoming the first quadriplegic at his level of ability to race an ultra-marathon of 325 miles between Salt Lake City and St. George, Utah.

Art is a great example of someone whose powerful positive attitude sustained him and empowered him, even when he went through one of the most devastating tragedies imaginable, and even though every day he has to live with the fact that he is disabled. "Pain comes to teach us," he says. "If we become frustrated, we've lost the lesson. When we see pain as having a purpose in life, it drives us closer to our dreams."

Art has taken what he has learned about the power of a positive attitude and dedicated himself to sharing it with others. "Before the accident, I was looking for a way to make a living," he said. "Since the accident, I've been looking for a way to make a contribution."

My friend's story is truly incredible, but I don't want to leave you with the impression that you have to have an extraordinary background to make a difference in this world. Just as every one of us has the power to choose an attitude that empowers us, each of us has the ability to reach out and empower and help others by sharing our gifts, no matter what they are.

Leaving a Lasting Legacy

My attitude was forever changed when I received a book and a letter from a gentleman whose name I have forgotten, unfortunately. We attended a self-development course together. In the letter, he noted that I had been a blessing to him throughout the three-day course, and he was sending the enclosed book, *See You At the Top* by Zig Ziglar, hoping it would be a blessing to me. That book was more than a blessing; I read that book over and over every day for a year. It helped change my attitude and ultimately helped change my life.

It was one of the first motivational books to enlighten me about the power of attitude. Many of the godly principles that were woven throughout the text made a tremendous difference in my life. I recently had the opportunity to attend a tribute for Zig Ziglar. More than a thousand people came to honor this humble man of God. Zig was one of twelve children from a Depression-era family in Yazoo, Mississippi. He became a successful salesman and then one of the top motivational speakers and authors in the country.

Zig has inspired millions throughout his career. When he was first asked if he would be willing to accept a tribute on his behalf, he was somewhat hesitant, but had a change of heart when he learned that all proceeds would be donated to the Living to Change Lives Foundation. It's a nonprofit organization that develops character-building programs for young people by teaching them the importance of attitude, goal setting, self-esteem, integrity, and leadership. The wave of recent school shootings and violence only underscores how important building character and leadership is today in our society. Zig has made a positive difference in many lives, but his involvement with the foundation is going to have an even greater impact. Through his work with young people, he is creating a lasting legacy that will benefit generations to come.

It doesn't matter where you're born, how much money you have, or what your educational level is. What matters is that you recognize you can make a difference and that God has a purpose for you.

Education Is the Foundation for Creating a Legacy

Nido R. Qubein came to this country from Lebanon more than twenty-six years ago as a teenager with fifty dollars in his pocket. He knew just enough English to get by. His dream was to work very hard and become a successful American citizen. Today he is one of the top business consultants and professional speakers in the country and President/CEO of Creative Service, Inc. in Highpoint, North Carolina.

Nido was blessed to have his college education paid for by an anonymous donor. He was so grateful that he passed that legacy on to others by forming the Nido Qubein Scholarship Fund. To date that fund has awarded more than four hundred scholarships and grants worth more than a million dollars. Nido believes that life is one-third earning, one-third learning, and one-third serving. My friend Nido is one of the most giving and caring people in the world. His attitude is making a difference and leaving a lasting legacy.

Education made a big difference in Nido's life, as it has in mine. We should all be thankful for the teachers who have made a difference in our lives. Unfortunately, many educators throughout the world are not getting the recognition they deserve. Many are underpaid, underappreciated, and overworked. Marva Collins was a teacher in Chicago's public schools for fourteen years before she left the district. She was frustrated by her experiences in the public school system and dissatisfied with the lack of quality education her own children were receiving at prestigious private schools. Marva established an educational program on the second floor of her home, and in 1975—with five thousand dollars and six children (two of her own)—she founded Westside Preparatory School in Chicago's Garfield Park.

In the first year, every one of the youngsters in her school increased their scores on standardized tests by at least five grades. What makes their phenomenal success more remarkable is that these children had been labeled "learning disabled, problem children, and borderline retarded."

Marva's success with youngsters labeled as "unteachable" by the school system led to an offer to serve as the U.S. Secretary of Education, but she declined in order to stay with her own school. She, like many teachers, is certainly making a difference and leaving a lasting legacy. The lives of hundreds and hundreds of young people have been changed for the better because of her belief that "every child is a born achiever."

It's important to know that we can all play a part in educating a child. You don't have to be in the classroom to be an educator. When retired phone company employee Don Kastle visited Fort Logan Elementary School in an impoverished neighborhood of Sheridan, Colorado, he was disturbed by what he saw. Students in tattered clothing, often without shoes, were working in a building that was all but falling apart. Teachers there had given up their annual raises to help cut costs, but the school was badly in need of repairs that the school board could not afford.

Kastle decided to adopt Fort Logan Elementary School. He enlisted fellow members of Telephone Pioneers of America, an organization for phone company retirees, in a campaign that collected clothing for the students of the school. They also collected thousands of dollars in used office equipment and computers from a local law firm. And the volunteers built a new playground for the students, who responded by behaving better than ever before. According to school officials, Kastle's effort made a difference. Kastle created a legacy by motivating volunteers who continue to come back each year.

I am thankful for Marva Collins and all the people who are committed to education. I pray and I hope that they never give up, because education is the foundation for all the legacies that have been and will be created in this world.

The Power of a Wish

The Make-A-Wish Foundation is making a tremendous difference in the lives of young people and their families. Its purpose is to grant wishes for children with terminal or life-threatening illnesses. The Make-A-Wish Foundation was founded twenty years ago when a small community of concerned friends and strangers came together to grant the wish of one little boy who wanted to be a police officer for a day. Since then it has grown to an organization with eighty-one chapters nationwide, eighteen international affiliates, and over thirteen thousand volunteers worldwide.

I had the privilege of being the keynote speaker at their national conference a couple of years ago. I did not fully understand the great work of this organization until I found myself in a ballroom with more than five hundred other people listening to a mother share her story of how one wish for her dying daughter had brought the family a moment of joy, happiness, and laughter.

Four-year-old Aaron Alexander was honored that day as the fifty-thousandth child to be granted a wish by the foundation. Aaron suffers from sickle cell anemia. On the day we met, he was running around getting into everything like a typical little boy. Aaron's wish had been to be a cowboy. Make-A-Wish flew him and his mother to the Selkirk Ranch in Dillon, Montana, where he dressed like a cowboy and worked alongside the ranch hands. A parade was held in his honor. His mother told me how much being a cowboy had changed her son's life. She said that before his wish was granted, Aaron would always complain about being tired and in pain, but since returning from Montana, he often runs around the house saying, "Mama, Mama, I'm a cowboy, Mama, Mama, I'm a real cowboy now."

Having an opportunity to speak at the Make-A-Wish conference and meeting Aaron showed me firsthand the power of fulfilling a child's wish. President and CEO Paula Van Ness said, "The power of the wish is that it creates moments of hope, strength, laughter, and dignity that improve the lives of our wish children, regardless of their medical condition. My vision is that one day everyone walking this earth will experience the life-affirming, life-altering, addictive, and exquisitely blessed power of a wish."

The Gift of Sight

For two consecutive years I've spoken at the LensCrafters Annual General Managers Meeting. They were among the most enthusiastic audiences I've had the pleasure of addressing. After meeting the former president and CEO, Dave Browne, I could easily understand why. The entire organization is committed to making a difference with their Gift of Sight program. Dave told me, "We make decisions with our heads and commitments with our hearts. Each one of our associates has made a decision and a commitment to our Gift of Sight program."

The program delivers free optical services to needy people in North America and around the world. On one designated day called Hometown Day, all LensCrafters stores in the United States and Canada open early to donate eye exams and eyeglasses to needy people in their communities.

I recently received a letter from Jay Scott Stoelting, executive director of LensCrafters Foundations. Scott shared a story about one Hometown Day recipient:

Our most memorable Hometown Day story is about a student we've never even met. We were almost finished delivering exams and free glasses to about twenty students from a local school when the teacher asked if we could repair the glasses of a student whose mother would not let her participate in the Hometown Day. When we opened the envelope containing her glasses we found the frame with lenses but no arms. The girl had taken twisted ties and looped them through the hinges, then connected a string through the ties, which she wore around her head. The teacher told us she had worn them to school every day despite her classmates' critical jokes. We were moved by this girl's situation and determined to replace her glasses. But when we discovered the prescriptions for her existing glasses were –8.25, –4.5, we all cried. What that means is that her vision was very, very bad. We chose a beautiful frame and made the new glasses, which her teacher delivered. Although we didn't see the girl's face when she received them, we had the satisfaction of knowing the gift of sight had made an incredible difference in her life.

This story illustrates that even when you cannot see the results of your work, you are still able to know in your heart that you made a tremendous difference in someone else's life. Don't ever forget that there are so many needs and so many ways in which you can make a difference.

An Attitude of Service

Marian Wright Edelman, a Yale Law School graduate and civil rights activist who founded the Children's Defense Fund, said, "Doing good for others is just the rent you pay for living on this earth." She's talking about taking on an attitude of service and turning that attitude into action by serving others, no matter who you are, where you are, or what you do. We all have time to serve if we make time, and we should all make time as long as we have time.

I was reminded of this while hearing a speech by Johnnetta Cole, former president of Spelman College and currently Presidential Distinguished Professor of Anthropology, Women's Studies, and African American Studies at Emory University. Dr. Cole is a dynamic woman who serves on a number of corporate and charitable boards. Yet in her speech she talked about making time in her incredibly busy schedule to mentor an eleven-year-old girl who's stolen her heart. While she thought she'd be the one enriching the young girl's life, she realized that they have a relationship based on mutual love, respect, and admiration.

We can all find the time to give back, because along our journeys there have been those special people who took the time with us. As Dr. Cole stated in her recent address, "Anybody can be great because anybody can serve. All you need to serve is a heart full of grace, and a soul motivated by love."

Make a Mark and Make a Difference

Four years ago, I was on the road speaking when I hit a wall. I was sitting on the bed of yet another hotel room, drained physically and mentally. I felt myself slipping into a negative attitude, and I did absolutely nothing to stop it. I picked up a room service menu and stared at the same entrees that I'd been staring at for twenty-four straight days on this road trip. I couldn't shake a nagging sense of dread and dissatisfaction.

I sensed that I was headed for a slight case of depression, so I yanked out the Attitude Tool Kit and started a tune-up: *Why am I feeling this way? I've got my own business. I've got a busy schedule. I've got a great staff. My books and tapes are selling all over the world. I'm making good money. I have a new house and a car. I have all the material things I ever wanted, and I'm pursuing my purpose and passion.*

The tune-up was going well, but then I dropped a wrench into the works. *So why do I feel so unhappy? I can hear myself complaining all the time about things that never bothered me before.*

I pulled the plug on my inner dialogue for the night, which you have to do sometimes when you know that weariness is pushing you into negative attitude territory. But the next day I still had a lot of negative nagging going on. It stayed with me until I met my cousin Gina for lunch in Chicago, and she told me that she was going to attend a service that evening by Dr. Creflo A. Dollar, Jr., the charismatic pastor. He began his church with eight members in an Atlanta elementary school and built it into the dynamic World Changers Church International in College Park, Georgia, which has a congregation of more than seventeen thousand people. His ministry is worldwide, with offices in Australia, Canada, South Africa, and the United Kingdom.

I was familiar with Pastor Dollar. I had watched him several times on television on the Trinity Broadcast Network and had even attended his church a couple of times, but I declined my cousin's invitation to go along. She tried to talk me into it, but I was feeling tired. After our lunch, I returned to my hotel room. My negative inner dialogue picked up where it had left off the previous night, so I pulled the plug again and took a nap. *Maybe I'm just road-weary,* I thought. Three hours had passed when I awakened. I felt energized, so I decided to join my cousin after all. When I arrived at the theater, I couldn't believe the number of people outside. There must have been at least five thousand standing in line to get in.

I overheard some people in the line saying that they'd driven nine hours to get there. Someone else responded, "There are a lot of people who've driven farther than that." Pastor Dollar's ten-thousand-seat church is fifty minutes from my home in Atlanta, and I'd only made the effort to drive to his services twice, I thought.

I walked down to the first row to see if I could find Gina, but there were too many people and she was nowhere in sight. Still, I wasn't worried. I felt comfortable there, more comfortable than I had in many weeks. I felt like something important was about to take place.

Transcending Self and Reaching Out

The youthful Pastor Dollar appeared on the stage to the applause of the crowd. He immediately began his sermon on the topic "Making a Mark That Cannot Be Erased." To make a mark, he explained, is to really make a difference in somebody else's life. Often, when you do that, it has a ripple effect. Your helping or guiding someone else touches many lives by virtue of having touched one. It's contagious.

It's important to understand that the smallest gesture can have a major and lasting impact on a person's life. We don't always know the outcome or how many lives we touch, but it's true beyond a doubt that when you extend a hand to one person, many others move forward.

When I first heard Pastor Dollar's words that day, they were channeled into my spirit. I realized that with all my negative internal dialogue, I had started to lose sight of my many blessings. I'd become self-centered and self-serving. In my road-weariness, I'd fallen into a pattern of boredom and self-pity. Sure, I was tired. Sure, traveling around the country can wear you out. But I'd lost sight of the fact that I was living my dream.

Pastor Dollar reminded me that my focus should be on showing my thankfulness to God for his gifts to me by developing them and sharing them. I connected with Pastor Dollar's vision when he talked about really making a difference and becoming a "world changer." That's when a light went on inside of me, and I realized that I needed to become a more spiritual being. Pastor Dollar asked the question "Who wants to profit in life?" We all raised our hands. He replied, "To profit, you must plant the word of God inside yourself. You must not only be a hearer of the Word, but a doer of the Word. There are sixty-six books in the Bible; sixty-six bags of seed that are the words of God. If you want your success; if you want to produce your harvest—you must plant those seeds."

I experienced a breakthrough that night, a major shift in perspective. It was at that moment I decided to rededicate my life to Christ. As a Christian, I wanted to do more than just carry the title. Instead of approaching the world from an attitude of *What's in this for me?* I embraced an attitude of *What can I do for God, and what can I do for others?* Pastor Dollar made me realize that I needed to view the world from an attitude of thankfulness and humility. I realized that the greatest rewards you can obtain in life are those that come when you forget about gathering rewards for yourself and instead look to create them for others. To be a world changer, you first have to change what is inside you.

I left the amphitheater that night with a renewed spirit and a new attitude, committed to making a mark that cannot be erased. Looking back on that night, I wonder what would have happened if I'd never taken the first step. I hate to think what my life would be like.

My goal for writing this book was to make a difference in your life so that you in turn will make a difference in the life of someone else, thus making a mark that cannot be erased. I believe you have greatness within you. Now it's time to let the rest of the world know. If you continually practice the steps outlined in the book, you'll notice a positive change in yourself and in the way people perceive you. Each day you have the choice to decide what type of day you're going to have.

As you go about the business of being a positive force in your own life and the lives of others, I ask that you take the time to let me know how you've been able to incorporate the ten life-changing steps into a plan of action. Feel free to write us at Harrell Performance Systems, Inc., Post Office Box 81268, Atlanta, GA 30366, or visit our website: www.super-fantastic.com.

God has given us all special gifts, but they are not for us alone. Our gifts are meant to bless the lives of others, and that's what making a mark is all about. Remember, your attitude is your most priceless possession. I wish you a super-fantastic journey in discovering the power and spirit that lives within you. *Attitude . . . is everything!*

In all that you get, get understanding.

—PROVERBS 4:7

For more information about Keith Harrell's broad range of services, including speaking, consulting, training, and published materials (cassettes and videos), please visit his website at: www.super-fantastic.com

INDEX